THE MILITARY EQUATION
IN NORTHEAST ASIA

STUART E. JOHNSON *with Joseph A. Yager*

THE MILITARY EQUATION
IN NORTHEAST ASIA

THE BROOKINGS INSTITUTION
Washington, D.C.

Library of Congress Cataloging in Publication Data:
Johnson, Stuart E   1944–
    The military equation in northeast Asia.
    (Studies in defense policy)
    Includes bibliographical references.
    1. United States—Armed Forces—East Asia.
2. East Asia—Defenses.   3. United States—Foreign
relations—East Asia.   4. East Asia—Foreign relations
—United States.   I. Yager, Joseph A., 1916–
joint author.   II. Title.   III. Series.
UA26.A842J63   355.03'305   78-20900
ISBN 0-8157-4689-X

9 8 7 6 5 4 3 2 1

THE BROOKINGS INSTITUTION is an independent organization devoted to nonpartisan research, education, and publication in economics, government, foreign policy, and the social sciences generally. Its principal purposes are to aid in the development of sound public policies and to promote public understanding of issues of national importance.

The Institution was founded on December 8, 1927, to merge the activities of the Institute for Government Research, founded in 1916, the Institute of Economics, founded in 1922, and the Robert Brookings Graduate School of Economics and Government, founded in 1924.

The Board of Trustees is responsible for the general administration of the Institution, while the immediate direction of the policies, program, and staff is vested in the President, assisted by an advisory committee of the officers and staff. The by-laws of the Institution state: "It is the function of the Trustees to make possible the conduct of scientific research, and publication, under the most favorable conditions, and to safeguard the independence of the research staff in the pursuit of their studies and in the publication of the results of such studies. It is not a part of their function to determine, control, or influence the conduct of particular investigations or the conclusions reached."

The President bears final responsibility for the decision to publish a manuscript as a Brookings book. In reaching his judgment on the competence, accuracy, and objectivity of each study, the President is advised by the director of the appropriate research program and weighs the views of a panel of expert outside readers who report to him in confidence on the quality of the work. Publication of a work signifies that it is deemed a competent treatment worthy of public consideration but does not imply endorsement of conclusions or recommendations.

The Institution maintains its position of neutrality on issues of public policy in order to safeguard the intellectual freedom of the staff. Hence interpretations or conclusions in Brookings publications should be understood to be solely those of the authors and should not be attributed to the Institution, to its trustees, officers, or other staff members, or to the organizations that support its research.

With the compliments of

Bruce K. MacLaury
President

THE BROOKINGS INSTITUTION
1775 Massachusetts Avenue, N.W., Washington, D.C. 20036

FOREWORD

The present deployments of U.S. military forces in Northeast Asia and adjacent waters reflect the problems of an earlier day. China, once seen as a prime threat to U.S. interests in the area, has been moving gradually toward cooperation with the United States. Though time has not softened the enmity between the two Koreas, South Korea has gained a clear economic lead and is growing in defensive military strength. Soviet naval strength in the western Pacific, having steadily increased, now poses a potential threat to Japan's vital sea lanes.

Taking such changes into account, the authors of this book, the twentieth in the Brookings Studies in Defense Policy series, evaluate the ability of U.S. forces in Northeast Asia to support current U.S. policy in that part of the world. They conclude that various shifts in deployments would yield a force better adapted to coping with today's problems and release some units to meet urgent needs elsewhere.

The authors received advice and assistance from many persons in the course of their work. They are particularly grateful for the helpful comments and suggestions of Barry M. Blechman, Rolf H. Clark, Ralph N. Clough, Evelyn S. Colbert, Andrew L. Cooley, Robert L. Day, Alfred K. Richeson, Philip H. Trezise, and Frederick W. Young.

Stuart E. Johnson, a former Brookings research associate, is now on the staff of R & D Associates. Joseph A. Yager is a senior fellow in the Brookings Foreign Policy Studies program.

The study was edited by Diane Hammond and checked for accuracy by Judy Cameron. Jeanane Patterson and Ann M. Ziegler provided secretarial services.

The Institution acknowledges the assistance of the Ford Foundation, whose grant helps to support its work in defense studies. The views presented in this book are solely those of the authors and should not be ascribed to the persons whose assistance is acknowledged above, to the Ford Foundation, or to the trustees, officers, or other staff members of the Brookings Institution.

BRUCE K. MACLAURY
President

October 1978
Washington, D.C.

CONTENTS

Tables

GLOSSARY

of terms and designations

A	Attack aircraft
Aegis	Surface-to-air missile system
AEW	Airborne early warning
AGM	Air-to-ground missile
APC	Armored personnel carrier
ARM	Antiradiation missile
ASM	Air-to-surface missile
ASDF	Air Self Defense Force (Japan)
ASW	Antisubmarine warfare
AWACS	Airborne warning and control system
B	Bomber
BADGE	Base air-defense ground environment (Japan's air-defense radar system)
C	Military transport aircraft
CG	Guided missile cruiser
CL	Light cruiser
CPIC	Coastal patrol and interdiction craft
CV	Diesel-powered aircraft carrier
CVN	Nuclear-powered aircraft carrier
DD	Destroyer
DDG	Guided missile destroyer
EA	Marine electronic warfare aircraft
F	Fighter aircraft
FF	Frigate
FFG	Guided missile frigate
GSDF	Ground Self Defense Force (Japan)
ICBM	Intercontinental ballistic missile
IRBM	Intermediate-range ballistic missile
LAMPS	Light airborne multipurpose system (helicopter)
LCU	Utility landing craft
LHA	Assault landing craft
LPH	Helicopter landing platform
LSD	Dock landing ship
LSM	Medium landing ship
LST	Tank landing ship
MIRV	Multiple independently targetable reentry vehicle
MRBM	Medium-range ballistic missile
MR/IRBM	Medium- or intermediate-range ballistic missile
MSDF	Maritime Self Defense Force (Japan)
NATO	North Atlantic Treaty Organization
P	Antisubmarine patrol aircraft
PRC	People's Republic of China
PSMM	Multimission patrol ship
PT	Motor torpedo boat
ROC	Republic of China
ROK	Republic of Korea
SAM	Surface-to-air missile
SDF	Self Defense Force (Japan)
SH	Antisubmarine helicopter

xi

SLBM	Submarine-launched ballistic missile	SSGN	Nuclear-powered guided missile submarine
SS	Diesel-powered attack submarine	SSM	Surface-to-surface missile
SSB	Diesel-powered ballistic missile submarine	SSN	Nuclear-powered attack submarine
SSBN	Nuclear-powered ballistic missile submarine	TOW	Tube-launched, optically tracked, wire-guided (antitank missile)
SSG	Diesel-powered guided missile submarine	V/STOL	Vertical or short takeoff and landing (aircraft)

CHAPTER ONE

INTRODUCTION

Northeast Asia ranks second only to Central Europe as the most heavily armed region of the globe.[1] The Soviet Union and the People's Republic of China have established a military standoff along the Amur and Ussuri Rivers dividing Manchuria and eastern Siberia. The two Koreas face each other across the cease-fire line, their relations marked by intense hostility and suspicion. The Republic of China, on the small island of Taiwan, has built a modern military establishment to defend itself against any attempt by Peking to liberate the only Chinese province outside its control. The Soviet navy routinely operates throughout the western Pacific and beyond, and its air forces conduct regular reconnaissance flights in areas surrounding Japan. Finally, the United States maintains a strong military presence in the area. Only Japan has chosen not to build a military establishment commensurate with its great economic and technological strength.

U.S. Interests and Goals

The U.S. interest in Northeast Asia remains what it was when American sailing ships first traveled to China: access for purposes of trade, investment, and other peaceful activities. Implicit in access to an area, of course, is peace in that area. Despite the continuity of these two interests, the goals pursued to achieve them have changed. Over a century ago, it was opening Japan to trade with the outside world. Later, the possibility that China would be divided into spheres of European influence became the major problem and led to the adoption of the open-door policy. Dur-

1. For purposes of this study, Northeast Asia includes Japan, North Korea, South Korea (Republic of Korea, or ROK), People's Republic of China (PRC), and the Republic of China (ROC). The Soviet Union is treated as a global power.

ing the first half of the century, the United States was concerned with Japanese military and naval power and with its efforts to gain control of China. Japanese aggression against China directly threatened U.S. access and was one of the reasons for U.S. involvement in World War II.

After Japan's surrender in 1945, U.S. concern shifted to the efforts of the Chinese Communists to overthrow the Chinese government, an ally of the United States in the war against Japan. The Communist victory on the China mainland in 1949 was followed in less than a year by the North Korean effort to reunify the Korean peninsula by force. U.S. support of South Korea was countered by Chinese forces supporting North Korea to block what China perceived as a threat to its own borders.

The military armistice in Korea in 1953 ushered in a period of frozen confrontation between the PRC and the United States that was to last for almost two decades, during which the U.S. goal in all East Asia was to contain the Communist threat to freedom of access. During the first part of this period the threat was seen as a joint Soviet-Chinese one, and the unmistakable evidence in the early 1960s of a split between the two Communist powers was not for many years reflected in U.S. goals.

In the early years of confrontation with the PRC, the United States made formal security commitments that still influence policies, although the way they affect the formulation of goals has subtly changed.[2] The first of these commitments was the mutual security treaty with the Philippines, which came into effect in 1952. This was followed by mutual security treaties with Japan (1952),[3] Australia and New Zealand (1952), the Republic of Korea (1954), the Republic of China (1955), and by the Southeast Asia Collective Defense Treaty (1955).

Although the confrontation ended in a formal sense with the visit of former President Nixon to China in 1972, many fundamental changes had already occurred. These changes, more than any single dramatic event, began the new era in Northeast Asia and helped reshape U.S. goals. Foremost among these changes are the rise of Japan to global importance as an economic power and the split between the PRC and the Soviet Union. Only slightly less important—and still not fully appreciated by the world at large—is the emergence of the Soviet Union as a major power in East

2. The treaties with the Philippines and with Australia and New Zealand were meant to provide against the resurgence of Japanese militarism. Their purpose, like the others, became the containment of communism.

3. This treaty was replaced in 1960 by the Treaty of Mutual Cooperation and Security Between the United States of America and Japan.

Asia and the western Pacific. These three developments are forcing the United States to fit its goals in Northeast Asia into a global context. One other change is the altered perceptions the United States and the PRC have of one another. The Vietnam War demonstrated that the United States was not seeking excuses to attack China and that China was not engaged in aggression by proxy in Vietnam.

In the new era in Northeast Asia, the interests of the United States are still access and peace. In contrast to the recent past, however, its goals are not containing a perceived political and military threat but are (1) maintaining Japan's international orientation, (2) improving relations with the PRC and the Soviet Union, (3) preventing forcible change in the territorial status quo in Korea and Taiwan, and (4) inhibiting further spread of nuclear weapons in the area.

Maintaining the international orientation of Japan is of prime importance. U.S. interests would suffer grave damage, globally as well as regionally, if Japan were to fall under a hostile government or under one that would detach it from the international trading system on which the welfare of the United States and other nations with free market economies depend.

U.S. Policies

Many of the actions taken by the United States in Northeast Asia are aspects of global policies. Thus, reducing barriers to trade with and investment in Northeast Asia is part of a wide effort to increase the benefits of international trade. Similarly, U.S. strategic forces deter nuclear threats against its allies in other areas as well.

But much of what the United States does in Northeast Asia is specific to that area. For this study it is useful to separate political and economic policies from security policies.

Political and Economic Policies

In Northeast Asia—and indeed in East Asia as a whole—the United States gives priority to cooperation with Japan. Ideally, this means that the United States would consult with Japan on questions of interest to both countries and that U.S. and Japanese policies with respect to these questions would be coordinated. Because both nations are global powers, at least in their economic interests and influence, consultation and coordination would not be limited to regional issues.

In practice, U.S.-Japanese cooperation falls short of the ideal. The countries are economic competitors as well as trading partners and political and military allies, and special interest groups push for policies counter to the cooperative ideal. (For example, U.S. labor and industry try to curtail imports from Japan and Japanese business tries to prevent foreign investment in their country.) Furthermore, the United States is in every sense a global power, and except in the economic dimension, Japan is not. Japan must import most of its food and energy; the United States is a net exporter of food and still obtains a large part of its energy from domestic resources. Japan relies on the United States to defend it against all military threats except very small-scale attacks; the defense of the United States is only marginally strengthened by Japanese bases.

It is not surprising, then, that the United States and Japan see some international problems differently. Recent examples include Japanese misgivings concerning the deep U.S. involvement in Vietnam and the lack of Japanese diplomatic support for U.S. aid to Israel during the Arab-Israeli war in October 1973. What is surprising is that, despite great differences in the situations of the two countries, relations have been generally good. And with a few notable lapses (including the failure of the United States to give Japan advance notice of the change in its China policy in 1972), cooperation between the two nations has been satisfactory.

Next to Japan, China bulks largest in U.S. relations with Northeast Asia. This results in part from China's sheer size, global political influence, and long-run economic potential. Two circumstances, however, increase China's importance. One is the bitter Sino-Soviet dispute. The other is the tension between the U.S. security commitments to the Republic of China and U.S. efforts to normalize relations with the People's Republic of China, which rules the China mainland.

The United States has adopted a policy of neutrality in the Sino-Soviet dispute. At the same time, there can be no doubt that the dispute has made it easier for the United States to carry out its policies in Northeast Asia and other areas. China would be less interested in improving relations with the United States if it were not concerned with the threat from the Soviet Union. Also, the Soviet Union would be able to apply greater political (and possibly military) pressure in Europe and the Middle East if it were relieved of the threat from China.

Reconciling its relations with the People's Republic of China and the Republic of China is one of the most difficult problems the United States has in Northeast Asia. The United States has not been willing to normalize relations with Peking and break relations with Taipei without an assurance from Peking that it will not try to change the status of Taiwan by force. Peking, for its part, insists that the future of Taiwan is purely a domestic Chinese matter and has refused to give the needed assurance.

Although present relations with the two Chinese regimes may be impossible to continue indefinitely, none of the parties appears to be under any pressure to seek an early resolution of the problem. The United States will continue to expand trade with Taiwan and investments on the island, and trade and cultural exchange with mainland China will presumably also continue.

Korea is less important to the United States than either Japan or China, but the problems that the United States faces there are not any less difficult. (The most serious, security, is taken up below.)

Politically, the United States is committed to the peaceful reunification of Korea. Any other position would place the United States in opposition to the strong sentiments of the Korean people, North and South. Reunification—peacefully or by force—is not, however, a practical goal for the foreseeable future. Moreover, the division of Korea satisfies at least the minimum requirements of all of the great powers with interests in Korea. Therefore U.S. policies are in fact directed toward the stabilization of the status quo. The principal justifications for these policies are that keeping South Korea in friendly hands contributes to the security of Japan and that a Communist takeover could cause Japan to question the value of its security ties with the United States.

In past years, economic aid to South Korea was a major means of supporting the status quo, but with the rapid growth of the South Korean economy, the need for concessional aid has dwindled. Today, the primary instruments of stabilization are the security measures that are discussed later in this book and the diplomatic support the United States gives South Korea in the United Nations and elsewhere. This support, however, no longer involves an effort to isolate the Communist regime in North Korea. With the concurrence of South Korea, the United States now favors UN membership for both North Korea and South Korea and would welcome international recognition of both regimes, following the German precedent.

Security Policies

The formal elements of U.S. security policy toward Northeast Asia have not changed in over twenty years: as was the case two decades ago, the United States is still committed under mutual defense treaties to the security of Japan, South Korea, and the Republic of China, and the United States still backs these commitments with conventional and strategic forces. The meaning and underlying purposes of the commitments, however, have changed, as have the political significance of the military forces behind the commitments and the type of military contingency with which those forces are designed to cope.

The U.S. commitments to Japan, South Korea, and the Republic of China—and the forces deployed in support of these commitments—were for many years part of an integrated system designed to contain communism and that extended from Japan and Korea through Taiwan and the Philippines. Japan was included for geographical reasons and to prevent revival of Japanese militarism. Today the U.S. security system in Northeast Asia is no longer fully integrated. The Republic of China, once the central link, does not have diplomatic relations with Japan and the Philippines and is the only country that continues to see the People's Republic of China as a threat to its security. Japan is no longer a potential danger but a valued ally to the United States. If the system has any remaining general significance it is as a sign of continued U.S. interest in the countries of the western Pacific and as a barrier—as much political as military—to the southward spread of Soviet influence.

U.S. security policy toward Japan has three aspects: (1) providing a nuclear "umbrella," which both protects Japan from nuclear threats by either the Soviet Union or the PRC and reduces the possibility that Japan will decide to acquire its own nuclear weapons; (2) maintaining bases in Japan, which would be of great value in the defense of South Korea and Japan (in the unlikely event of a conventional attack on Japan), and which reassure the Japanese of the reliability of the U.S. commitment; (3) deploying naval, air, and ground forces in and around Japan, which insulate it from possible Soviet coercion. Japan is more comfortable in its present international alignment if it regards itself surrounded by U.S. rather than Soviet power. Since the nuclear aspect is part of a strategic balance that goes far beyond Northeast Asia, it is outside the focus of this book. Problems associated with the bases and the deployment of forces, however, are relevant.

Military bases cause friction with the local population and potential disagreement with the Japanese government over use of the bases for purposes other than the defense of Japan. The first problem is inevitable and is not unique to the U.S.-Japanese relationship. And, except possibly on Okinawa, where good land is scarce and the concentration of U.S.

forces is heavy, the problem seems to be manageable, at least in the near term. Over the longer run, however, the United States cannot count on keeping all its present bases in Japan, and the day might well come when all its bases will have to be relinquished.

By agreement with the United States, Japan has what amounts to the right to veto the launching of combat operations from U.S. bases except those required for the defense of Japan. As a practical matter, the United States could not use the bases for even noncombat purposes associated with military operations in other areas if the Japanese authorities objected. For many years the United States regarded its bases in Japan as potentially available to support operations in fulfillment of U.S. security commitments in Southeast Asia as well as in Northeast Asia. (The bases on Okinawa, which at the time had not been returned to Japanese administration, in fact performed an important supporting role for U.S. forces in Vietnam.) With the withdrawal of U.S. forces from mainland Southeast Asia, however, the only areas that could be protected by the bases are South Korea and Taiwan.

The present Japanese ruling party would very likely approve the use of the bases to help repel a clear-cut North Korean attack on South Korea. However, if responsibility for the outbreak of hostilities were not clear, approval would be less likely; and if a coalition government that included elements from opposition parties came into power, its reaction to even unambiguous North Korean aggression could not be predicted with any degree of confidence.

Even the present Japanese government is unlikely to allow the United States to use its bases in Japan to support operations—either combat or noncombat—in the defense of Taiwan. Japan does not recognize Taipei and has diplomatic relations with Peking. More fundamental, Japan does not want to be drawn into a military confrontation with China.

Current U.S. security policies toward China contain a fundamental contradiction. On the one hand, the United States is committed by formal treaty with the Republic of China to resist an armed attack on Taiwan, an island over which both the Republic of China and the People's Republic of China claim jurisdiction.[4] On the other hand, the United States

---

4. The Mutual Defense Treaty Between the United States and the Republic of China reads: "Each Party recognizes that an armed attack in the West Pacific Area directed against the territories of either of the Parties would be dangerous to its own peace and safety and declares that it would act to meet this common danger in accordance with its constitutional processes" (6 UST 433).

has moved to improve its relations with the PRC and cannot fail to recognize that its overall military posture in Northeast Asia is a major reason this effort has achieved some success. This is so because the PRC regards the U.S. presence as a barrier to the spread of Soviet influence. Thus the United States is, simultaneously, interposing a major obstacle to the PRC's goal of "liberating" Taiwan and providing a political and psychological counterweight against the PRC's enemy, the Soviet Union.

Paradoxically, either an improvement or a worsening of Peking's relations with Moscow could cause security policy problems for the United States. On the one hand, even a partial healing of the Sino-Soviet dispute could lessen the value to Peking of good relations with the United States, leading it to invite a military confrontation over Taiwan, which would force the United States to decide what its obligations are under the mutual defense treaty with the Republic of China. On the other hand, increased tension between Peking and Moscow, possibly leading to hostilities, would raise the question of whether the United States should try to strengthen Peking and, if so, how. Current policy does not appear to take explicit account of this contingency. With respect to the first, security policy seems to be to strengthen Republic of China's forces (through sales of defensive military equipment) in the hope they might deter or repel attack without U.S. assistance.

The security policy of the United States toward Korea is, quite simply, to deter a North Korean attack against South Korea, thereby giving South Korea the security essential to political stability and economic growth. For more than twenty years the means of deterrence have been the mutual defense treaty with South Korea, the U.S. military forces deployed in South Korea and nearby areas, and the assistance provided to South Korea in its efforts to modernize its own forces.

The major question for the future is whether the United States should continue to station forces in South Korea. The arguments for and against continuing the deployment of the various kinds of forces are presented in detail in subsequent chapters. It is sufficient to note here that the considerations are complex and involve political and psychological as well as military judgments. Moreover, the impact on Japan of possible changes in U.S. deployments may be as important as the impact on South and North Korea.

A security problem that affects all countries in the area is the possible proliferation of nuclear weapons. China is now the only nuclear-weapons power in Northeast Asia, and the policy of the United States is to discourage the acquisition of such weapons by any of the other nations. Nonproliferation is a complex subject and extends beyond the scope of this book. There is, however, a connection between other U.S. security policies in Northeast Asia and the attitudes of at least the non-Communist countries toward the acquisition of nuclear weapons. To the extent that the United States makes those countries feel secure, it reduces the likelihood they will try to acquire nuclear weapons. Each of the three —Japan, South Korea, and the Republic of China—is different, however, and factors other than U.S. security policies will enter into their decisions on nuclear weapons.

CHAPTER TWO

MILITARY FORCES

In Northeast Asia, U.S. military forces face no immediate challenge from a major adversary across a well-defined front. The relationships among the various powers in this part of the world are complex and the military environment amorphous. Before policy can be related to problems in such an environment, the deployment and operating patterns of the military forces of the region need to be understood.

The Soviet Union

Although less than 10 percent of the population of the Soviet Union is found east of Irkutsk, about 25 percent of Soviet conventional forces in 1977 were there:[1]

Ground divisions	Aircraft	Ships
37 motorized rifle	600 (P-VO Strany)	7 cruisers
5 tank	300 (Naval Aviation)	53 destroyers and frigates
1 airborne	1,200 (Frontal Aviation)	24 submarines armed
	200 (Long Range	with cruise missiles
	Aviation)	45 submarines armed
		with torpedoes

Ground Forces

The forty-three Soviet divisions stationed in the military districts near China and in Mongolia are an increase of nearly one-third over the thirty stationed in the region before the deterioration in Sino-Soviet relations

1. Robert P. Berman, *Soviet Air Power in Transition* (Brookings Institution, 1978), pp. 39, 41, 43, 44; Barry M. Blechman and Robert P. Berman, eds., *Guide to Far Eastern Navies* (Naval Institute Press, 1978), pp. 31, 50; International Institute for Strategic Studies, *The Military Balance, 1977–1978* (London: IISS, 1977), pp. 8–9.

Table 2-1. Soviet Army Divisions Bordering China and in Central and Eastern Europe, 1977

Type of division	Tanks per division	Personnel per division	Divisions bordering China	Divisions in Central and Eastern Europe
Motorized rifle	188	11,500	36	15
Armored tank	316	9,000	5	16

Sources: International Institute for Strategic Studies, *The Military Balance, 1977–1978* (London: IISS, 1977), p. 9; U.S. Department of the Army, Headquarters, *Handbook on Soviet Ground Forces* (Government Printing Office, 1975), pp. 4–9, 6–21, A-3, A-10.

highlighted by the border tensions of 1969. After reaching forty-four divisions in 1972, the deployment has remained roughly constant.

That the large Soviet deployment in the eastern military districts is oriented toward China is beyond question. How these forces might be employed and how long it would take them to prepare for combat is in dispute. Most of the twenty-two divisions in the military district of the Far East, which borders on Manchuria, are maintained near the border. In men and firepower they match, crudely, Chinese strength in Manchuria. Moreover, many are in a relatively low state of readiness, only about a third being at or near full combat strength. (By comparison, all of the Soviet divisions in East Germany are maintained at full combat strength.) Soviet divisions in Asia also tend to be more lightly equipped than those in Europe. (The composition of divisions bordering China and those in Central and Eastern Europe is shown in table 2-1.) Even so, the concentration of Soviet armor is far heavier than the armor of Chinese troops across the border.

As early as 1973 it was reported that the Soviet Union was building barracks, roads, rail spurs, accommodations for families, and permanent training grounds in the Far East,[2] seeming to indicate an intention to continue to station a strong force in the area. A preemptive strike by this force would almost certainly require moving strong reinforcements into the area and bringing the assigned divisions to greater combat readiness. (For example, during the four months preceding the Soviet invasion of Manchuria in August 1945, 750,000 men were moved into the region from the Western Front.)[3]

2. International Institute for Strategic Studies, "Will the Soviet Union Attack China?" *Strategic Survey 1973* (London: IISS, 1974), p. 66.

3. William Fowler, "Russia's War Against Japan," *Marshall Cavendish Illustrated Encyclopedia of World War II,* vol. 22 (London: Marshall Cavendish, 1972), p. 3000.

Table 2-2. Landing Craft, Soviet Far East Fleet, 1977

Type	Number	Capacity (tons)	Capacity (tanks)	Year built
Ropucha-class LST	1	1,000	20	1976
Alligator-class LST	4	1,700	20–30	1966
MP-2/4/6/8-classes LCU	10	150–500	4–8	1956–60
MP-10-class LCU	10	150	4	1959–66
Vydra-class LCU	35	250	4	1967–69
Polnocny-class LSM	12	350	6	1963

Sources: Barry M. Blechman and Robert P. Berman, eds., *Guide to Far Eastern Navies* (Naval Institute Press, 1978), p. 51; John E. Moore, ed., *Jane's Fighting Ships, 1977–78* (London: Macdonald and Jane's; and New York: Jane's Yearbooks, 1977), pp. 712–15.

Furthermore, Soviet ground forces in the Far East are not configured so that large forces could be sent far from their present locations. The forces along the Manchurian border include only one airborne division that, at full strength, consists of only 7,000 men (about half the size of a motorized rifle division), and seems designed to operate as a strategic adjunct to larger forces of armored and motorized divisions.[4] Moreover, no tanks are assigned to the division (because Soviet capability for heavy airlift is scant), limiting the division's use in offensive operations except when it is part of a larger, heavier force.

Not all Soviet troops in Northeast Asia are on the Chinese border. One motorized rifle division is headquartered on Sakhalin just across the Soya Strait from Hokkaido (the northernmost Japanese island). Troops are also deployed on the Kamchatka Peninsula and on some of the Kuril islands. These troops "train for landings, repulsion of enemy landings and mutual reinforcement of mainland forces."[5]

The Soviet naval commands also maintain ground forces, 12,000 men trained for the amphibious mission (similar to the U.S. Marine Corps). Amphibious equipment is divided roughly equally among the four fleets.[6] Assuming that the manpower is also divided equally, the complement in the Far East Fleet would be 3,000 men, or perhaps one brigade. Even if the naval infantry were augmented by army forces, their ability to get across water is limited by poor amphibious-lift capability (see table 2-2),

4. Jeffrey Record, *Sizing Up the Soviet Army* (Brookings Institution, 1975), p. 12.

5. Japan Defense Agency, *Defense of Japan 1976* (Tokyo: Japan Defense Agency, 1976), p. 16.

6. Robert Berman, "Soviet Naval Strength and Deployment," in Michael Mcc-Gwire, Ken Booth, and John McDonnell, eds., *Soviet Naval Policy* (Praeger, 1975), p. 422.

which seems suited only for lifting a task force of modest size to a nearby objective.

Naval Forces

The Soviet navy is divided into four fleets, three of which (the Black Sea Fleet, the Baltic Sea Fleet, and the North Sea Fleet) are deployed in waters off the western border of the Soviet Union. The Far East Fleet, with headquarters at Vladivostok, has traditionally operated off the Soviet eastern maritime provinces; it now also deploys submarines carrying strategic ballistic missiles to waters off the West Coast of the United States and maintains a small force of ships in the Indian Ocean.

After World War II, development of the Soviet Far East Fleet concentrated on area defense. Its thirty-five small craft (*Osa*-class), capable of speeds of thirty knots and armed with antiship cruise missiles, are supplemented by land-based aircraft and fixed cruise missile launchers. Together, they pose a severe problem to enemy surface ships operating near Soviet naval installations. Antisubmarine warfare (ASW) capability is provided by numerous coastal patrol craft, older conventional attack submarines, and ASW aircraft and helicopters. Many of the old frigates and destroyers are designed for antisubmarine warfare in home waters. Air defense is provided by land-based surface-to-air missiles and P-VO Strany aircraft. This force, which is concentrated in the Sea of Japan, seems to be directed not at offensive operations toward Japan but at defending naval installations at Vladivostok and Nakhodka against possible U.S. attack.

Following the pattern for the rest of the Soviet navy, most new equipment in the Far East Fleet can operate over longer ranges and for longer periods away from base than the older ships. The fleet has deployed forces and participated in exercises far from its bases, in areas where it could threaten Western interests.

Its force of major surface combatants has remained at roughly sixty over the past five years, while the fleet has gradually been modernized. A number of *Skory*-class destroyers and *Riga*-class frigates, built in the 1940s and 1950s, have been retired. In addition to problems stemming from age, these ships lacked the modern armaments of the Soviet warships now entering service which, while not equaling the numbers of those retired, expand the fleet's operating range. Its most capable ships in this regard include three *Kresta*-class cruisers, three *Kotlin-SAM*-class destroyers (an increase of one since 1970), and two modern *Krivak*-class destroyers, which recently appeared in the Pacific. Neither the Soviet navy's newest cruiser nor the *Kiev*-class V/STOL aircraft carrier has as yet appeared in the Pacific.

On the whole, two trends are apparent in the surface fleet: modernization (which has extended the fleet's ocean-going capability), and emphasis on antisubmarine warfare (although all of the larger ships carry some antiship and air-defense armament as well). It cannot be determined from an examination of equipment alone whether the primary concern is U.S. ballistic missile submarines, or Chinese or U.S. attack submarines.

About a third of the total Soviet submarine force is assigned to the Far East Fleet, including twenty-three ballistic missile submarines (seventeen of them nuclear-powered). Some of them are deployed in the eastern Pacific in position to strike targets in the continental United States.

The remaining sixty-nine submarines are available for attack. Until the mid-1960s, almost all attack submarines were conventionally powered, noisy, and limited in range. Today, the fleet has thirty-one nuclear-powered attack submarines. Four *Charlie*-class and fourteen *Echo II*-class nuclear-powered submarines (SSGNs), armed with antiship cruise missiles, form the core of the force. The *Charlie*-class submarines can launch SS-N-7 missiles with a range of about fifty kilometers while remaining submerged. But to target a U.S. aircraft carrier, they must penetrate the carrier's protective ASW screen. The *Echo II*s and other cruise missile submarines must surface before launching their missile, the SS-N-3 Shaddock (maximum range approximately 600 kilometers). Six diesel-powered cruise missile submarines (SSGs) supplement this capability. Although the number of cruise missile submarines has not grown in the past five years, four nuclear-powered submarines have replaced four diesel-powered models, giving greater range and firepower. Soviet cruise missile submarines are configured and operated primarily to strike U.S. aircraft carriers, although they could, of course, threaten any surface ship.

A smaller force of thirteen nuclear-powered attack submarines are designed primarily for use against other submarines. These include four modern *Victor I* class, four older *November* class, and five *Echo I* class. The primary weapon is the torpedo. This force is augmented by thirty-two diesel-powered patrol submarines (SSs), the fourteen *Foxtrots*, with ten torpedo tubes each, being the most capable. The others—four *Zulus,* two *Bravos,* and twelve *Whiskeys*—are most useful for coastal patrol and training.

Lacking aircraft carriers, the Soviet Far East Fleet includes about 335

Table 2-3. Aircraft, Soviet Naval Air Force, Far East Fleet, 1977

Type	Number	Combat radius (kilometers)	Description
Tu-16B/C/G	85	2,500–3,000	Medium-range bomber with antiship missiles
Tu-16D/E/F	45	2,500–3,000	Reconnaissance aircraft
Tu-22	15	1,000	Reconnaissance aircraft
Tu-20	20	6,000	Reconnaissance and antisubmarine aircraft
BE-12	10	2,000	Antisubmarine seaplane
Il-38	15	3,600	Antisubmarine aircraft
MI-4, MI-14, KA-25, MI-8	145[a]	500–2,300	Antisubmarine helicopters

Sources: Robert P. Berman, *Soviet Air Power in Transition* (Brookings Institution, 1978), p. 43. Jean LaBayle Couhat, "Combat Fleets of the World 1976–1977," *Aviation Week and Space Technology*, January 24, 1977, p. 44.

a. Numbers for these aircraft vary depending on source.

land-based aircraft. These represent about 30 percent of all Soviet Naval Aviation resources and include both fixed-wing and helicopter aircraft. The Far East Fleet component is summarized in table 2-3.

The primary aircraft, the Tu-16 Badger (including reconnaissance, electronic warfare, and tanker versions), fills both strike and support roles. In the strike role, the Tu-16 can carry two antiship cruise missiles, including the AS-5 Kelt missile, which has a range of some 300 kilometers.[7] The Tu-16 was first produced in the middle 1950s; it flies at subsonic speeds and is not capable of low-altitude approach. It requires fighter escorts to survive hostile interceptor aircraft. The Tu-22 Blinder can fly at supersonic speeds; some models are configured to carry AS-4 Kitchen antiship missiles. It has a severely limited range, however, and has been rated unsuccessful by U.S. naval intelligence.[8] Helicopters, primarily KA-25 Hormone types, operate from both land bases and from *Kresta*-class cruisers.

The headquarters of the Far East Fleet is Vladivostok, located on the Sea of Japan near the mouth of the Ussuri River. Vladivostok is also the terminus of the trans-Siberian railroad and is the largest urban center in the eastern Soviet provinces. Additional naval facilities are located at nearby Nakhodka. Ships operating from these two bases compose the

7. William Green and Gordon Swanborough, *The Observer's Soviet Aircraft Directory* (London and New York: Frederick Warne, 1975), pp. 212–14.

8. Norman Polmar, "Soviet Naval Aviation," *Air Force*, vol. 59 (March 1976), p. 70.

Table 2-4. Shipdays, Soviet and U.S. Ships in Pacific Ocean, 1974–76

| Year | Shipdays | | Ratio of Soviet to U.S. ships |
	Soviet ships	U.S. ships	
1974	7,400	34,800	1.0:4.7
1975	6,800	27,000	1.0:4.0
1976	5,200	19,700	1.0:3.7

Source: U.S. Department of the Navy, Office of the Chief of Naval Operations, *Understanding Soviet Naval Developments* (GPO, 1978), p. 14.

Fifth Fleet, or southern group, of the Far East Fleet. Other bases serve the Soviet Seventh Fleet, or northern group. These are Sovetskaya Gavan (opposite Sakhalin), Korsakov (on the southern tip of Sakhalin), Magadan (on the northern shore of the Sea of Okhotsk), and Petropavlovsk (on the Pacific Ocean coast of the Kamchatka Peninsula). Development of the major base Petropavlovsk reflects an attempt to disperse operations of the fleet away from Vladivostok, where access to the open ocean is restricted to four narrow (and thus easily obstructed) straits bordering Japanese territory. (The narrow strait between the northern end of Sakhalin and the mainland provides in theory a fifth exit, but it is closed in winter by ice and even when not frozen cannot safely be transited by submerged submarines.) Petropavlovsk, the only base on the Pacific itself, now has extensive harbor facilities but lacks any road or rail link with the Soviet mainland and must be supplied by surface ships from Vladivostok. The focus of its operations is submarine deployments, primarily ballistic missile submarines.

After a growth of activity beginning in 1970, in part in response to U.S. naval operations in Southeast Asia, the Soviet presence in the Pacific appears to have stabilized at about 5,000-6,000 shipdays (see table 2-4). Activities of the support ships (oilers, tenders, oceanographic survey ships, and so on) account for a large portion of the total Soviet shipdays. In 1976 the Soviet Far East Fleet registered 700 combatant deployments in the Pacific, the U.S. Navy, 14,600. Indeed, of all the fleet areas of the Soviet navy—the Pacific, Atlantic, Mediterranean, and Indian Ocean—the Pacific area has the lowest combatant deployment: an average of two combatants per day in 1976, compared to twelve, twenty-five, and eight days, respectively, for the other regions.[9]

9. For an account of combat deployments, see U.S. Department of Defense, Office of the Secretary of Defense, "U.S. Defense Perspectives, Fiscal Year 1978" (Department of Defense, January 1977).

Table 2-5. Shipdays, Soviet and U.S. Ships in Indian Ocean, 1974–76

Year	Shipdays		Ratio of Soviet to U.S. ships
	Soviet ships	U.S. ships	
1974	10,500	2,600	4.0:1.0
1975	7,200	2,800	2.6:1.0
1976	7,300	1,400	5.2:1.0

Source: See table 2-4.

The Soviet presence in the Indian Ocean (after a surge in 1972 following the Indo-Pakistani conflict and port-cleaning operations in Bangladesh) has dropped somewhat and may have leveled off to about 7,000 shipdays (see table 2-5). In 1976, there were 2,900 Soviet combatant deployments and 1,500 U.S. combatant deployments. The greater Soviet combatant presence in the Indian Ocean, compared to the Pacific, is accounted for largely by a task force that uses berths in the region.

The expanded Soviet naval activity in the Pacific was highlighted in the Okean and Vesna exercises, in which ships from the Far East Fleet participated in maneuvers involving elements of the entire Soviet navy.[10] During Okean, in April 1970, twenty surface ships and twelve submarines from the Far East Fleet staged antisubmarine and antiaircraft exercises. Maneuvers included penetration into the Indian Ocean and amphibious landings in the vicinity of Vladivostok. A task force sailed south as far as the Philippines.

Vesna (usually called Okean II or Okean 75 in the West), in April 1975, involved more ships and broader operations. A primary aim of the exercise seems to have been to test the Soviet ocean surveillance network under realistic conditions in areas of potential interest to the Soviet navy. Included were interception and direction-finding by both shipborne and shore-based installations, air and surface surveillance, and satellites employing electronic intercept, radar, and photographic data-gathering (the last being of limited value since it does not provide information quickly enough for tactical operations). Another general aim of the exercise was

10. Details of the Okean and Vesna exercises are taken from the testimony of Rear Admiral B. R. Inman, U.S. Navy, Director of Naval Intelligence, in *Fiscal Year 1977 Authorization for Military Procurement, Research and Development, and Active Duty, Selected Reserve and Civilian Personnel Strengths,* Hearings before the Senate Committee on Armed Services, 94 Cong. 2 sess. (GPO, 1976), pt. 10, pp. 5316–27; Russell Spurr, "Moscow: Drawing the Asian Battle Lines," *Far Eastern Economic Review,* October 31, 1975, pp. 26–30.

to coordinate air strikes by Soviet Naval Aviation and Long Range Aviation against surface ships.[11]

In the Pacific, four task forces operated during Vesna. One force participated in heavy ASW activity near Petropavlovsk. Another formed a simulated convoy of four merchant ships and two auxiliaries escorted by a destroyer and sailed to the east of Japan. This convoy was attacked repeatedly from the air and possibly by submarines as well. An amphibious force approached the Straits of Tsushima and was attacked by submarines and aircraft. A task force also maneuvered in the vicinity of the Caroline islands. Finally, in a departure from previous operating patterns, a task force was reported to have deployed into the Yellow Sea and then south toward Taiwan. Among other firsts in this exercise was the attention paid to convoy and anticonvoy activity east of Japan, indicating possible interest in the vital sea lane linking the United States and Northeast Asia.

The Okean exercises took place in the context of broad expansion of operations by the Far East Fleet. In September 1971, a task force of seven combatants (a missile cruiser, two destroyers, three submarines, and a tanker) deployed within sight of the Hawaiian islands and conducted five days of ASW exercises before departing.

Expanded operations in the Indian Ocean may have been motivated by several considerations. First, petroleum shipments from the Persian Gulf to the West and to Japan transit the Indian Ocean. Second, U.S. ballistic missile submarines operate in these waters. And third, China has influence in the region and the Soviet Union may have wanted to bolster Soviet allies such as India. The more modest expansion in the Pacific perhaps reflects its limited opportunities for port calls by the Soviet fleet.

Air Forces

Soviet air power in the Far East is divided among Naval Aviation (discussed above); P-VO Strany, which has responsibility for defending military targets and civilian and industrial areas from air attack; Frontal Aviation, which supports operations of ground forces in combat areas by attacking enemy ground targets and by defending against attacking aircraft; Long Range Aviation, which trains and equips for long-range and strategic attacks; and Air Transport Aviation, which is responsible for airlift of troops and supplies.

11. Long Range Aviation is primarily responsible for deep-strike missions against ground targets; its secondary mission is to strike against seaborne targets.

Soviet aircraft in Northeast Asia are numerous and varied, forming a large, flexible force. As more sophisticated aircraft—with more demanding maintenance and higher price tags—enter the force in large numbers, the total number of aircraft is likely to decrease.

The most important installations to defend are the harbor and the industrial and military complexes of Vladivostok and environs. Modernization of P-VO Strany in this region includes the deployment of the MiG-25P Foxbat interceptor, which is capable of speeds of Mach 3 at high altitude or, alternatively, low-altitude flight at subsonic speeds.[12] The largest component of the force is still older-model aircraft, however—the Su-9, Su-11, and the MiG-19. The air defenses around Vladivostok are supplemented by fixed surface-to-air missile installations. The air defense forces, with their overlapping antiaircraft capabilities, would make air strikes against Vladivostok installations a costly undertaking in terms of aircraft lost.

Frontal Aviation is integrated closely with the ground forces. Its strength was doubled during the late 1960s and early 1970s, part of the buildup of Soviet forces on the border with China. It, too, is beginning to modernize, and recently adopted the Su-19 and MiG-23. These aircraft have greater ordnance-carrying capacity and longer ranges than those being replaced. But, again, most of the force is older-model aircraft, the MiG-21 being the most numerous.

Although Long Range Aviation aircraft are assigned to a specific theater, in time of conflict they can be deployed to strike the targets deemed important. Present deployments indicate that about one-fourth of the total force is prepared to strike targets in China. It has participated in maritime training operations, as well. The Tu-26 Backfire, recently introduced into Long Range Aviation command in the Far East, enhances the command's ordnance-carrying capability, range, and survivability.

Strategic Nuclear Capabilities

The Soviet Union maintains a considerable strategic nuclear arsenal: approximately 1,500 intercontinental ballistic missiles (ICBMs) and a fleet of about 82 ballistic missile submarines with capacity to launch some 900 nuclear missiles.[13] Adoption of the proposed Strategic Arms

12. See Berman, *Soviet Air Power,* for characteristics of the most recently deployed aircraft in Northeast Asian theater.

13. IISS, *The Military Balance 1977–1978,* p. 8.

Limitation Talks agreement would not greatly change the size of the Soviet strategic nuclear forces.[14] Development of such a large strategic nuclear capability is of course driven by global military competition with the United States.

As confrontation with China has intensified and as the Chinese have developed a nuclear weapons delivery capability, however, a portion of the Soviet arsenal has surely been allocated to cover targets in China. How great a portion is difficult to estimate. Although a fourth of the Soviet conventional forces are allocated to Northeast Asia, the fraction of its strategic nuclear forces allocated to Far Eastern targets is probably smaller. For example, although twenty-three of the eighty-two ballistic missile submarines in the Soviet navy are assigned to the Far East Fleet, their primary mission is to cover targets in the United States. It is also unlikely that a large fraction of the more than 1,500 Soviet ICBMs have been diverted from their primary purpose (strategic parity with the United States) to be targeted on China.

However, even a small fraction of the Soviet strategic nuclear capability directed at China would be a formidable threat. The missiles deliver a much greater payload than anything China possesses. The largest, the SS-18, can deliver one warhead with a yield of up to fifty megatons or a package of eight independent warheads.[15] (One megaton equals the explosive power of 1 million tons of TNT. The bomb dropped on Hiroshima had a yield of 0.015 megaton, or the equivalent of 15,000 tons of explosive power.) Submarine-launched ballistic missiles have warheads with a yield of one to two megatons. And the Soviet missiles are accurate. The latest generation of Soviet ICBMs is estimated to hit within one-third of a mile from the target. Maximum ranges are about 12,000 kilometers for the latest ICBMs and 7,700 kilometers for the latest submarine-launched missile.[16]

Finally, the Soviet Union has some capability to defend against a limited nuclear strike. An antiballistic missile system, including early warning radars and interceptor missiles, has been deployed around the periphery of Moscow.

14. For details of the Strategic Arms Limitation Talks, see U.S. Department of State, Bureau of Public Affairs, "The Strategic Arms Limitation Talks," Special Report no. 46 (July 1978).

15. Doug Richardson, "World Missiles Directory," *Flight International,* vol. 111 (May 14, 1977), pp. 1350–51.

16. IISS, *The Military Balance, 1977–1978,* p. 77.

China

The People's Republic of China concentrates its resources at the extremes of military technology. It gives priority to the development of a nuclear force based on high-technology ballistic missile delivery. However, the equipment provided the People's Liberation Army (the name for the army, navy, and air force, collectively) is unsophisticated and obsolescent, derived mostly from Soviet military technology of the 1940s and 1950s. The PLA, particularly the three-million-man army, draws its strength from the sheer size of deployments:[17]

Ground divisions	*Aircraft*	*Ships*
128 infantry	5,200 air force fighters	22 destroyers and escorts
12 armored	700 navy fighters	66 submarines (65 armed with torpedoes)

Ground Forces

The Chinese army is the largest in the world. It has three million active troops, which can be augmented by about 100 infantry-division equivalents of local forces under regional command.[18] However, only twelve active divisions are armored, and their heavy military equipment is largely obsolescent. Table 2-6 shows the ratio of armored vehicles to troops in comparison to the ratios of the United States and the Soviet Union. Relative to these industrially advanced superpowers, the Chinese army is built around the infantry soldier. This composition reflects the Chinese economy, with its huge reservoir of manpower and limited technological and heavy industrial resources.

The offensive potential of the PLA is therefore limited to the pace of a foot soldier and in both offense and defense by its lack of armored protection against artillery and automatic weapons. The PLA is also poorly

17. Ibid., pp. 53–54.
18. Description of the capabilities of the PRC ground forces is derived largely from *Allocation of Resources in the Soviet Union and China—1975,* Hearings before the Subcommittee on Priorities and Economy of the Joint Economic Committee, 94 Cong. 1 sess. (GPO, 1975), pt. 1; Russell Spurr, "China's Defense: Men Against Machines," *Far Eastern Economic Review,* vol. 95 (January 28, 1977), pp. 24–31; R. D. M. Furlong, "China's Evolving National Security Requirements," *International Defense Review,* vol. 9 (August 1976), pp. 557–62, 661; U.S. Defense Intelligence Agency, *Handbook on the Chinese Armed Forces,* DDI-2680-32-76 (DIA, July 1976).

Table 2-6. Personnel and Armored Vehicles in Armed Forces, People's Republic of China, Soviet Union, and United States, 1977

Country	Personnel (thousands)	Armored vehicles		Ratio of personnel to armored vehicles
		Tanks	Personnel carriers	
People's Republic of China	3,250	10,000	3,500	241:1
Soviet Union	1,825	43,000	47,000	20:1
United States	789	11,600	22,000	23:1

Source: IISS, *The Military Balance, 1977–1978*, pp. 5, 8, 9, 53.

equipped to defend against an armored thrust by a highly mechanized force. The Chinese possess none of the new antiarmor guided missiles present in large numbers in U.S. and Soviet units.

The PLA also lacks mobility, with too few trucks to make rapid deployment by road possible and a rail network inadequate to compensate. Deployment of forces is thus very significant, since the brunt of an attack would be absorbed by the units in place. Only two of the thirty-seven field armies are in the Foochow military region, which includes Fukien province opposite Taiwan. A force this size could not overwhelm Taiwan, although it is adequate to deter forays by Nationalist troops stationed on nearby Quemoy and Matsu islands. An invasion of Taiwan would require a substantial redeployment of PLA forces to this region.

The heaviest deployment is in the northeast (fourteen field armies are in the Shenyang and Peking military regions), reflecting China's concern over the large Soviet deployment in eastern Siberia and its own need to protect the industrial heartland of Manchuria and the capital. China's tactic against the superior armor and mobility of the Soviet forces is to engulf and drown the advancing enemy in a sea of defenders. Given the equipment and present deployment of the PLA, no other style of defense is feasible. The troops in Manchuria are not equipped to mount a forward defense against a concerted armored thrust and more troops are stationed in the Peking military region than in Manchuria itself. In other words, the Chinese are prepared only for a defense in depth, in which temporary loss of territory would be tolerated until the invader is worn down.

Air Force

The Chinese air force resembles the Soviet air force of the 1950s in equipment and organization: an air force tailored for defense. Its poor

Table 2-7. Tactical Aircraft in Air Force, People's Republic of China, 1977

Type[a]	Number	Combat radius[b] (kilometers)	Ordnance capacity[b] (tons)	Description
Shenyang F-9	300	800	0.5	Fighter-bomber
MiG-15	300	280	0.5	Fighter-bomber
MiG-17	1,500	520	0.5	Interceptor
MiG-19	2,000	980	0.5	Interceptor
MiG-21	120	550	0.5	Interceptor
Il-28	400	1,020	1.1	Light bomber

Sources: IISS, *The Military Balance, 1977–1978*, pp. 53–54; U.S. Defense Intelligence Agency, *Handbook on the Chinese Armed Forces*, DDI-2680-32-76 (DIA, July 1976), Annex Z.
a. Chinese-built aircraft may differ from their Soviet-built counterparts.
b. Authors' estimates based on sources.

range and low payload limit its ability to carry the battle far from its operating bases (see table 2-7). The interceptor force has received over 90 percent of China's approximately 5,200 combat aircraft, but its mainstay fighters, the MiG-17 Fresco and the MiG-19 Farmer, are products of Soviet technology of the late 1940s and the 1950s. The Chinese MiGs carry only 0.5 ton of ordnance, while the Soviet MiG-23 Flogger can carry two tons of ordnance, the Su-19 Fencer five tons, and the U.S. A-10, sixteen tons.[19] Numbers can compensate for some of the shortcomings of individual aircraft and air combat armaments, but numbers alone cannot compensate for inadequate defense against aircraft penetrating at low altitude, inadequate defense against attack at night or during low-visibility weather conditions, and a poor system of early warning against air attack.

The interceptor force is supplemented by surface-to-air missile (SAM) installations concentrated around Peking and a few other key urban/industrial areas, particularly in the northeast.[20] China's only SAM is the CSA-1, basically a copy of the Soviet SA-2 Guideline, and it is not effective against aircraft flying at low altitude.[21] Investment seems to have gone into antiaircraft guns (37–100 millimeters), but they are an old Soviet design with only limited capability against high-performance aircraft. The air-defense surveillance and control network consists of ground-based radar sites. More sites are being constructed, indicating that China has not yet reached the basic coverage it seeks.

19. Charles M. Gilson, "Military Aircraft of the World," *Flight International*, vol. 111 (March 5, 1977), pp. 558–59, 576–77.
20. *Allocation of Resources in the Soviet Union and China—1975*, Hearings, pt. 1, p. 114.
21. An additional SAM, a land-based variant of the missile carried by the *Kiangtung*-class frigate, may well exist. This missile is possibly an unlicensed copy of the Soviet SA-3 GOA (Doug Richardson, "Missile Forces of the World," *Flight International*, vol. 112 [November 26, 1977], p. 1598).

China's tactical bomber force is built around Il-28 Beagle light bombers and some MiG-15 Fagot aircraft configured for ground strike operations. Both are of late 1940s Soviet design. The MiG-15 lacks the range, payload, speed, avionics, and ordnance of modern attack aircraft, which limits its effectiveness and its ability to survive against modern air defenses. The Il-28 can carry a substantial ordnance load and has a wide combat radius, but it is slow (maximum speed 0.8 Mach) and vulnerable to interceptor planes and ground-based defenses.

Although China has shown interest in modernizing its air force, its aircraft industry has neither adequate research and development capability nor access to the latest Soviet or Western technical expertise.

The most modern aircraft to have an extended production run is the MiG-19, which began licensed production in 1959. Attempts to copy the MiG-21 apparently were unsuccessful, since production halted in 1975 after fewer than 100 were placed into service.[22] More recently, China developed the Shenyang F-9 based on its MiG-19 but with all-weather radar and an engine with higher thrust and greater reliability. But these improvements are not significant, overall, and production is proceeding slowly.[23]

There are obstacles to China's receiving assistance from the Western aerospace industry in upgrading its air force. The United States, the leader in military aircraft technology, does not yet sell military equipment to China (which would have serious repercussions on U.S. relations with Moscow). Moreover, advanced military aircraft are expensive and China's foreign exchange earnings are low. However, Great Britain has given China a license to produce the Rolls-Royce Spey engine (used to power the British F-4 Phantom), which may mean China will eventually produce an advanced fighter aircraft designed for this engine. Also, China is interested in buying Harrier V/STOL (vertical or short takeoff and landing) attack aircraft from Great Britain.[24] These aircraft's ability to take off and land on austere fields seems suited to a people's war, for, like ground forces, they can disperse throughout the countryside and harass the invader. Providing logistical support for such an operation would be extremely difficult, however.

22. Nikolai Cherikov, "The Shenyang F-9 Combat Aircraft," *International Defense Review,* vol. 9 (October 1976), p. 714.

23. Ibid., p. 716.

24. Furlong, "China's Evolving National Security Requirements," pp. 561, 661.

Naval Forces

China's navy is the third largest in the world, much larger than the British and French navies combined, growing from a few dozen vessels in 1949 to slightly over 1,700 ships. A simple count overstates the capability of the fleet, however, for most are small, relatively inexpensive vessels designed for coastal patrol, and the inventory of major combat ships remains small (see table 2-8).

The *Romeo* and *Whiskey* submarines are of 1950s design, slow, noisy, diesel-powered ships, limited in range and in staying power away from base. They risk detection in operations in the open ocean against a navy with modern ASW capability. They are a valuable component of coastal defense, however, where neither speed nor endurance are crucial.

The surface combatants are a mix of Soviet models from the 1940s and 1950s (*Gordy* and *Riga*) and Chinese models built recently (*Kiangnam* and *Luta*) but patterned after Soviet ships of 1950s vintage. These ships have good sea-keeping characteristics and sufficient range to operate away from China's coastal waters. The largest, the *Luta* class, has a range estimated at 7,400 kilometers, adequate for operations in waters off Southeast Asia or in the Philippine Sea, and its six antiship cruise missiles would make it a powerful antishipping instrument.

Open-ocean operations seem to have a low priority in the PRC navy, however. The navy has not developed an adequate force of auxiliary ships to provide logistic support to the fleet. Since it must rely on shore-based

Table 2-8. Combat Ships in Navy, People's Republic of China, 1977

Type	Number	Displacement[a] (*tons*)	Primary weaponry
Submarine			
Romeo-class SS	42	1,600	Torpedo
Whiskey-class SS	21	1,180	Torpedo
Ming-class SS	2	1,500	Torpedo
Destroyer			
Luta-class DDG	5	3,250	Antiship cruise missile
Gordy-class DDG	4	1,660	Antiship cruise missile
Frigate			
Riga-class FFG	4	1,200	Antiship cruise missile
Kiangtung-class FFG	1	1,800	Antiship cruise missile
Kiangnan-class FF	5	1,350	ASW rocket, guns

Sources: Moore, ed., *Jane's Fighting Ships, 1977–1978*, pp. 87–89; IISS, *The Military Balance, 1977–1978*, p. 53.

a. Dived displacement for submarines; standard displacement for surface ships.

logistic support, the surface fleet cannot conduct sustained operations. Moreover, it has little ASW capability and primitive air-defense weapons so in operations beyond the protection of land-based aircraft would be vulnerable to air or submarine attack.[25] (However, the navy did launch a successful offense several hundred miles from port when it seized the Paracel Islands from South Vietnamese forces in 1974.)

The naval air arm gives the fleet air defense and antiship capability. About 500 MiG-17s and MiG-19s provide defense cover for a few hundred miles out to sea. They are no match individually for modern high-performance aircraft, nor do they effectively defend against antiship cruise missiles or aircraft attacking at low altitude. A limited antiship capability is provided by 100 bombers, mostly obsolete Il-28s configured to carry torpedoes.

The Chinese amphibious force is small and largely obsolete. The tank landing ships (LSTs) are the only landing craft with a capacity greater than 1,000 tons. These craft are World War II vintage U.S. vessels captured from the Nationalists in 1950. Fifteen at most are still operational.[26]

The Chinese have a strong coastal defense based on diesel-powered attack submarines and a large contingent of small coastal patrol craft. The most capable are the missile boats, which are like the Soviet *Osa* and *Komar* classes—small, fast, and maneuverable. They are armed with the CSS-N-1, the Chinese version of the Soviet Styx antiship cruise missile. Construction of these ships appears to have high priority, and the present force of 140 is reported to be expanding. About 675 small vessels, whose primary armaments are torpedoes, guns, and depth charges, round out the coastal defense force. Their maximum speeds vary from thirty to fifty knots. Because of their relatively primitive armament, they are individually less effective than the missile patrol craft.

Nuclear Capability

The development of a nuclear capability commands high priority in the allocation of China's scarce technical resources. Building on technical aid from the Soviet Union (provided before 1960), China was able to ex-

25. *United States–Soviet Union–China: The Great Power Triangle,* Hearings before the Subcommittee on Future Foreign Policy and Research and Development of the House Committee on International Relations, 94 Cong. 1 and 2 sess. (GPO, 1976), pt. 2, p. 185.

26. John E. Moore, ed., *Jane's Fighting Ships 1977–78* (London: Macdonald and Jane's; and New York: Jane's Yearbooks, 1977), p. 93.

plode a nuclear device by 1964, to fire a nuclear-tipped ballistic missile by 1966, and to detonate a hydrogen bomb by 1967.

China today deploys thirty to forty medium-range ballistic missiles (MRBMs), designated CSS-1.[27] The missile resembles early Soviet systems: it is of limited range (about 1,100 kilometers) and its accuracy is poor. It is transportable from one site to another and can be targeted at points about China's periphery. It delivers a relatively small warhead, about twenty kilotons.[28]

An intermediate-range ballistic missile (IRBM), designated CSS-2, has been operational since 1972; thirty to forty are deployed at present.[29] The missile has a range of 2,800 kilometers, sufficient for strikes against targets in eastern and central regions of the Soviet Union. It carries a one-megaton warhead, fifty times larger than that of the CSS-1, although small compared to the larger Soviet missiles (the SS-18 can deliver a fifty-megaton warhead). Moreover, the accuracy of the CSS-2 is poor, which further limits its effectiveness relative to Soviet or U.S. missile systems.[30]

A new missile, the CSS-3, was flight-tested in 1976. It has a range of 5,500 kilometers, bringing some targets in European Soviet Union within reach. Only a few are currently operational, however.[31] Work is underway on the CSS-X-4; with a range of about 13,000 kilometers, it is a true intercontinental ballistic missile. Deployment of the CSS-X-4 would give China the capability to strike a target anywhere in the Soviet Union and almost anywhere in the United States. Deployment of these systems is proceeding slowly, and operational capability is not expected for several years.[32]

China also maintains a force of about sixty Tu-16 Badger bombers, which are capable of delivering nuclear weapons. Native production of the Tu-16 has ceased, and it appears it is being supplanted by the less-capable Il-28, also configured for nuclear delivery.[33] The Il-28 lacks both the range and the ability to penetrate modern air defenses, requirements

27. IISS, *The Military Balance, 1977–1978*, pp. 52–53.

28. Defense Intelligence Agency, *Handbook on the Chinese Armed Forces*, p. 8-1.

29. IISS, *The Military Balance, 1977–1978*, p. 53.

30. Defense Intelligence Agency, *Handbook on the Chinese Armed Forces*, p. 8-2.

31. Richardson, "Missile Forces of the World."

32. *United States–Soviet Union–China*, Hearings, pt. 2, p. 183.

33. *Allocation of Resources in the Soviet Union and China—1975*, Hearings, pt. 1, pp. 113–14.

of strategic bombing missions. The bomber force is essentially regional, capable of only short-range attacks on targets about China's periphery.

China has one Soviet-designed *Golf*-class submarine, capable of carrying ballistic missiles, but it is not known whether such missiles have been developed.[34]

Japan

Following World War II, Japan's military forces were completely disbanded. The constitution adopted in 1946 included Article IX, which renounces war as the sovereign right of the nation and declares that "land, sea, and air forces as well as other war potential will never be maintained."[35] The constitution however, like any formal document, is subject to varying interpretations. In 1950, when almost all the U.S. troops garrisoning Japan were committed to Korea, the National Police Reserve Force was formed with responsibility for maintaining internal order. From this force evolved the Self Defense Force (SDF), whose primary role is to defend Japan from direct external aggression. Four five-year plans have been executed to expand and equip the SDF to the standards of a modern defense force.

The constitutional restraint, the lack of public support for expansion of the SDF, and the security provided by the U.S.-Japanese Mutual Security Treaty, have combined to keep Japan's military forces from growing in proportion to its economy and influence in the modern world.[36] Japan has held to a policy of allocating less than 1 percent of its gross national product to defense spending, an extremely low figure for an industrialized nation. By comparison, the United States spends about 6 percent of its gross national product on defense, the Soviet Union about 12 percent, and even Switzerland, with its long tradition of neutrality, spends 2 percent.[37]

In 1976 and 1977 Japan issued outlines of the nation's defense policy

34. Moore, ed., *Jane's Fighting Ships 1977–78*, p. 89.

35. An official translation of the Constitution of Japan appears in Dan Fenno Henderson, ed., *The Constitution of Japan: Its First Twenty Years, 1947–1967* (Seattle and London: University of Washington Press, 1968), appendix, pp. 301–15.

36. In a survey commissioned by Japan's Defense Agency, only about 17 percent of the respondents felt the SDF should be expanded. Japan Information Service, *Japan Report* (New York: Japan Information Service, May 1976), p. 2.

37. IISS, *The Military Balance, 1977–1978*, pp. 82–83.

in preparation for budgetary requests in coming years.[38] Under these plans, the SDF will remain modest in size, and defense will rest on the security treaty with the United States—under which aggression against Japan will automatically involve U.S. military forces (including strategic nuclear forces, if the situation should warrant). This risk is a powerful deterrent to aggression against Japan.

The policy of joining with the United States to deter aggression is meaningful only in the context of close coordination between the SDF and U.S. forces. To this end, then U.S. Secretary of Defense James R. Schlesinger and Japan Defense Agency Director General Michita Sakata met in August 1975 to establish a committee to achieve closer U.S.-Japan defense cooperation. In July 1976, the U.S.-Japan Defense Cooperation Subcommittee met for the first time.[39] The inauguration of this committee reflects a realization that the United States no longer has an unchallenged military advantage in the western Pacific. Japan's armed forces, though modest in size and deficient in some key areas, have become an important supplement to U.S. forces in providing a homeland defense. (Japan has ratified the nuclear nonproliferation treaty and possesses no nuclear weapons.)

The Self Defense Force is organized into ground, air, and maritime components. In 1977 their deployments were:[40]

Ground	*Air*	*Maritime*
12 infantry divisions	90 F-4EJs	45 destroyers and frigates
1 mechanized division	160 F-104Js	15 submarines armed
	100 F-86Fs	with torpedoes
		130 ASW patrol aircraft

Its basic strength is to be sufficient to repulse limited aggression quickly.[41] The emphasis is on a balanced force, held in a high state of readiness.

Ground Force

The Ground Self Defense Force (GSDF), now 155,000 men, was created in 1954 from the Police Reserve Force, which had grown from 75,000 to 130,000 men. Almost all of the additional troops were stationed

38. Japan Defense Agency, *Defense of Japan 1976* and *Defense of Japan 1977*.
39. Japan Defense Agency, *Defense of Japan 1977*, pp. 122–23. The Subcommittee is a subordinate organ of the Japan-U.S. Security Consultative Committee.
40. IISS, *The Military Balance, 1977–1978*, pp. 59–60.
41. Japan Defense Agency, *Defense of Japan 1977*, p. 58.

in Hokkaido, reflecting a concern about Soviet forces in the maritime provinces, on Sakhalin, and on the Kuril islands.

The Self Defense Forces are lightly equipped—about 740 tanks and 500 armored personnel carriers, or one armored vehicle per 125 troops. While the army is more heavily equipped than China's (with one armored vehicle per 241 troops), it is far lighter than other industrialized nations. The Soviet army averages one armored vehicle per twenty troops, the United States one per twenty-three troops; West Germany one per thirty troops, and Britain one per twenty-six troops.[42] While the need for heavily armored forces is less urgent for Japan than for these nations (since troops attacking Japan must come by air or sea, which limits their firepower), Japanese troops without the cover of armor would be extremely vulnerable to strikes from artillery and from the air. Sustained air strikes would, at the very least, inhibit their ability to maneuver.

Ground force equipment is being modernized. About 150 battle tanks of Japanese design type 74 have been built. Type 74 draws upon the features of modern tanks of other nations and is of comparable capability to foreign front-line tanks. However, most of the tank force (560 tanks) are type 61, whose firepower, mobility, and armor are inferior to its U.S. prototype, the M-48, which has been phased out of service in the U.S. Army.

Japan has developed a new 155-millimeter artillery unit and a multiple rocket launcher. Both systems are self-propelled, both have armor protection for the crews, and their addition to the force in numbers would enhance significantly the firepower of the GSDF. However, by 1976 only twenty of a planned purchase of ninety had been procured, and procurement of the rocket launcher just began in 1977.[43] Budgetary constraints may well limit use of these systems to a level too modest to contribute meaningfully to the GSDF's firepower.

Four of the thirteen GSDF divisions are stationed in the north, including its one mechanized division. These units are at a higher level of readiness and better equipped than the GSDF as a whole. In 1974, an independent tank unit, the First Tank Brigade, was formed and it, too, was stationed in Hokkaido. The remaining GSDF units are distributed throughout the islands, with no particular priority given to western Japan near Korea, in part, no doubt, because of the strong U.S.-South Korean forces on the Korean peninsula.[44]

42. IISS, *The Military Balance, 1977–1978*, pp. 5, 8–9, 19, 53, 59.
43. Japan Defense Agency, *Defense of Japan 1976*, p. 92.
44. Japan Defense Agency, *Defense of Japan 1977*, app. 36.

The GSDF also operates eight Hawk surface-to-air missile groups, which provide local air defense against aircraft approaching at low and medium altitudes. Each group has twenty-four launchers with three missiles each. Two groups are in Hokkaido and two in the west, according a slight priority to the areas of Japan most accessible by air from the Kurils and the Asian mainland.[45]

In August 1975, Secretary of Defense James Schlesinger singled out the GSDF logistic system as an area where improvement was needed.[46] During the four defense buildup plans, resources were concentrated in equipping the combat arms elements of the GSDF, and the support units did not develop apace. The thin logistics support restricts the GSDF's ability to fight a sustained conflict. In addition, mobility is weak and cannot give timely reinforcement of units under attack. Finally, the size of the GSDF is declining; non-NCO enlisted personnel is about 70 percent of authorized strength.[47]

Air Force

The Air Self Defense Force (ASDF) is responsible for preventing intrusions into and adjacent to Japan's airspace. The defense is organized around the Base Air Defense Ground Environment (BADGE) air control and warning radar system. This network, with twenty-eight sites throughout Japan, simultaneously monitors all aircraft above and around the four main islands. If unidentified aircraft approach Japanese airspace, fighter aircraft on constant alert are scrambled to intercept the unidentified aircraft, taking their guidance from the appropriate radar site. Scramble time is short (less than five minutes, typically) and the number of ASDF scrambles was about 300 scrambles a year until 1976, when the number jumped to about 500.[48]

The ASDF maintains 10 active fighter squadrons: four of F-4EJs, and six of F-104Js. The most capable fighter in Japan's forces is the F-4EJ, a version of the U.S. Phantom produced in Japan under license. There are 90 in active service; the force is programmed to expand to about 120. The largest portion of the force is the F-104J Starfighter. It is a supersonic aircraft but has poor low-altitude intercept capability and is outclassed by modern fighter aircraft in dogfighting capability. This fighter is being

45. Ibid., pp. 63, 73.
46. *Asahi Shimbun,* November 18, 1975.
47. Japan Defense Agency, *Defense of Japan 1977,* app. 17, p. 155.
48. Ibid., p. 154. For a description of the ASDF, see ibid., pp. 68–72.

replaced in several NATO air forces by the F-16; Japan plans to phase the F-104J out of service beginning in the early 1980s.[49] The F-86F, a U.S. aircraft of Korean War vintage, is a subsonic daylight-only fighter. It is being phased out of active service and is now used only for training.

Both the radar network and the aircraft are becoming obsolescent. BADGE's poor tracking of low-flying targets was illustrated in August 1976 when a defecting MiG-25 penetrated Hakodate Air Base in Hokkaido.[50] It could be expected to have difficulty monitoring any low-altitude overflights of the Soviet Tu-26 Backfire-B bomber. Moreover, none of Japan's fighters have good low-altitude intercept capability, even if they were vectored into the vicinity of the intruding aircraft.

In its recent proposed budget the ASDF requested the E-2C Hawkeye airborne early warning aircraft, which can detect and track aircraft approaching at low altitude, especially over water. The Japan Defense Agency had given up procurement of ten to fifteen aircraft in fiscal year 1978 but is asking for the aircraft in the 1979 budget.[51] The ASDF has selected the F-15 Eagle as its next mainstay fighter and plans to buy 100 beginning in 1979.[52] The F-15 has a lookdown radar, which allows it to track and intercept low-flying aircraft, and is a match for any Soviet aircraft. In addition Japan is building a Japanese-designed attack aircraft, the FS-T2, which can be configured with short-range antiship missiles. However, procurement is proceeding slowly (only twenty-six of a planned sixty-eight were procured through 1976) and at present Japan's strike capability is slight.[53]

Maritime Force

Japan's maritime defense capabilities remain modest despite the fact that the nation is most vulnerable to military aggression or coercion from the sea. An island nation with meager natural resources, Japan has developed an economy critically dependent on a generous inflow of fuel, raw materials, and food, and on open access to world markets. To carry out its two-way trade, Japan has built the world's largest merchant fleet,

49. See Barry Wheeler, "World's Air Forces 1978," *Flight International,* vol. 114 (July 8, 1978), p. 128, for an account of the ASDF's plans.
50. For an account of the incident, see Japan Defense Agency, *Defense of Japan 1977,* pp. 125–40.
51. Wheeler, "World's Air Forces 1978," p. 128.
52. Ibid.
53. Japan Defense Agency, *Defense of Japan, 1976,* p. 92.

dependent on a network of shipping lanes with long ocean transits. Free access to surrounding waters is also vital for Japan's fishing fleet, the largest in the world. Although not as vulnerable as extended shipping lanes, fishing rights are likely to continue to be a source of friction with the Soviet Union. In addition, potentially rich petroleum reserves off the Senkaku islands (Tiao Yu Tai), southwest of Okinawa, may involve Japan in contention with China.

Any one of these situations seems adequate motivation to develop major naval forces, but Japan has not. Though the risk of unfavorable foreign reaction is generally given as the reason, an unwillingness to spend the money is probably the real reason. The government did not even complete its four defense buildup plans, which included a modest expansion of the navy. Acquisition of fifty-four ships was programmed for fiscal years 1972–76, but only thirty-seven were procured, including eight of thirteen destroyers and three of five submarines.[54] This shortfall bears little relation to a low naval profile: it was a time of high inflation and poor economic performance, and the MSDF budget simply presented a place where savings could be made.

Another reason Japan has kept its naval force down is the security provided by the U.S.-Japanese Mutual Security Treaty. U.S. naval might makes the threat from the Soviet Union seem less formidable. Japan provides port and overhaul facilities at Yokosuka for the U.S. Seventh Fleet, which serves to wed the interests of Japan and the United States in the western Pacific.

All of the major ships in its Maritime Self Defense Force (MSDF) are of Japanese design and construction. Most of the ships are designed for the ASW mission. The most capable of these are the modern *Haruna*-class helicopter destroyers (two now in service, two under construction). The three helicopters on board each *Haruna* extend ASW coverage, increasing the probability of detecting a hostile submarine before it comes within lethal range. These destroyers also have an antiaircraft missile system.

Another modern class of destroyer, the *Amatsukaze*, is entering service. It has, in addition to a modern ASW suite, a modern air-defense missile system. Two have been commissioned and a third is under construction.

The other forty-one destroyers and destroyer escorts in the MSDF are

54. Ibid.

roughly comparable to ships of other modern navies in ASW capability. However, the MSDF has no fighter aircraft for fleet air defense against either aircraft or antiship cruise missile attack. (The ASDF, which might provide air coverage for the fleet, must already stretch its limited resources to defend the home islands.) Air defense missiles and electronic counter-measures equipment could be retrofitted onto many of these destroyers, but budgetary constraints have eliminated this option. The fleet also lacks modern antisurface ship weaponry, and its surface combatants would be at a severe disadvantage in battling surface ships of most modern navies, which are so armed.

The fifteen submarines of the MSDF are all diesel-powered. Five—of the *Ooshio* class—are short range and most appropriate for coastal de-fense. Ten are capable of long-range missions, five of them (*Uzushio* class) having the modern teardrop hull design (for underwater maneuver-ability) and advanced bow-mounted sonars.

The MSDF supplements the fleet's ASW capability with a force of about 130 land-based ASW aircraft. As nuclear propulsion and improved hull designs have made modern submarines increasingly more quiet, how-ever, this force has become increasingly obsolescent. Even the most mod-ern component in the force, the seventy-seven Kawasaki P-2J aircraft, has limited capability against modern submarines. The MSDF has entered into a contract to procure forty-five Lockheed P-3Cs (the most capable ASW aircraft operated by the U.S. Navy).[55]

In sum, the Japanese maritime defense operates modern ships and is maintained in a relatively high state of readiness. Its concentration on ASW to the exclusion of fleet air defense limits its ability to operate where hostile aircraft or ships armed with antiship cruise missiles are present, but even then, the ships could be effective as an adjunct to a more capable fleet, such as the U.S. Seventh Fleet.

Republic of China

The Republic of China's (ROC's) armed forces evolved from the Na-tionalist troops that withdrew from the mainland in 1949 and were subse-quently reorganized under the direction of Chiang Kai-shek. Most of their military equipment had been left on the mainland, and the Republic

55. Wheeler, "The World's Air Forces 1978," p. 128.

of China had neither the industrial base nor the financial resources needed to reequip them. At the outbreak of the Korean War, however, the United States began to extend military aid to Chiang Kai-shek. His forces were organized and trained along U.S. lines and provided with U.S. military equipment. At first, the items transferred were largely U.S. surplus equipment, but during the last decade they have included the latest generation of military hardware. The following table summarizes the strength of the ROC forces:[56]

Ground forces	*Aircraft*	*Ships*
18 infantry divisions	110 F-5A/B/E	28 destroyers and frigates
2 armored divisions	63 F-104s	5 submarines armed with
2 marine divisions	90 F-100A/D	torpedoes
2 airborne brigades	9 ASW patrol	3 ASW patrol boats
2 armored cavalry regiments	aircraft	14 coastal gunboats

Ground Forces

The military personnel who regrouped around Chiang Kai-shek on Taiwan were mainly from the army, and because of both inertia and the political influence of army officers, the army has retained its prominence despite the island's pressing naval and air defense requirements.

Of the total of 460,000 armed forces personnel, over three-fourths are in the army. Between 80,000 and 100,000 persons—mostly army— are stationed on the islands of Quemoy and Matsu, just off the coast of mainland China and opposite the ports of Amoy and Foochow, respectively. Quemoy, within artillery range of the mainland, is honeycombed with underground fortifications to provide cover for the defenders. Tanks, armored personnel carriers, and heavy artillery are deployed on the islands, along with supplies estimated to be adequate to ride out a six-month siege. Resupply and reinforcement of the islands during hostilities would be extremely costly, if not impossible.

On Taiwan itself, the road and rail network is extensive and rapid movement of troops about the island for reinforcement would be relatively easy, barring effective air strikes against key bridges. The tank force of 150 medium tanks (M-47/48) and 1,000 light tanks (M-41) is adequate to match that of an invading force, which would have to come by air or over water.

56. IISS, *The Military Balance, 1977–1978*, pp. 57–58; Moore, ed., *Jane's Fighting Ships, 1977–78*, p. 279; Wheeler, "World's Air Forces 1978," p. 111.

Air Force

In providing military equipment to the Republic of China, the United States has maintained a policy of emphasizing defensive weapon systems —or at least weapon systems of limited offensive potential. This is particularly evident in the aircraft supplied to the Nationalist air force.

Their most modern aircraft is the U.S.-designed-and-built F-5, which is a very capable interceptor but too limited in range and ordnance-carrying capacity to be very effective as a bomber. Over 100 F-5s—including about thirty F-5Es, the most modern version—have been supplied by the United States, and additional F-5Es are being assembled from U.S. components at the Aero Industry Development Centre in central Taiwan. The F-5E force is likely to grow to 300 aircraft as obsolete aircraft still in service or in reserve are retired.[57]

Sixty-three F-104 Starfighter aircraft are maintained, primarily for defense against attacking aircraft. Although designed over twenty years ago, it is a useful interceptor against the older model Soviet aircraft that account for most of the PRC air force. The ninety F-100 A/D fighter-bombers provide a capability to bomb targets on the mainland. They are even older than the F-104s, and the problems of maintaining an aging fleet should result in their being phased out of service by the early 1980s.[58]

Additional air defense is provided by two battalions (seventy-two launchers) of Nike-Hercules and one battalion (twenty-four launchers) of Hawk surface-to-air missiles.[59] A sophisticated radar air defense network will improve early warning of attacking aircraft and improve coordination of the command and control of missile batteries and interceptor aircraft.

Naval Forces

All of the major components of the ROC navy—its five submarines, eighteen destroyers, and ten frigates—were retired from the U.S. Navy and are more than thirty years old.

Eight of the destroyers were extensively remodeled by the United States in the 1960s, and four of these were equipped with Asroc (a one-to-six-mile range rocket-launched homing torpedo). The other four have ASW

57. Wheeler, "World's Air Forces 1978," p. 111.
58. Ibid.
59. IISS, *The Military Balance, 1977–1978,* p. 57.

suites roughly comparable to 1960s vintage U.S. equipment. In addition, seven of the eight have helicopter platforms, providing a potential for adding helicopter-based ASW systems, thereby enhancing detection probability and range of coverage. The remaining ten destroyers have not been extensively modernized, and their obsolescent ASW equipment and antiship cruise missiles make the whole destroyer force particularly vulnerable to sea attack—until the Gabriel antiship missiles Taiwan has ordered from Israel are in place. The Gabriel can operate in all kinds of weather and has a range at least comparable to the Soviet-designed missile used by mainland China.[60] Defenses against attacking aircraft, however, will remain poor. As a result, the destroyer force must depend on the ROC air force for all air defense.

The destroyer force is complemented by ten frigates. These ships are slower than the destroyers (about twenty knots maximum speed versus thirty-five knots), have less capable ASW armament, and lack modern antiaircraft defenses.

The ROC's five U.S.-built diesel-powered submarines, launched toward the end of World War II, were modernized in 1950. During hostilities they can patrol the coast but are too few for significant interdiction and attack. Coastal defense is augmented by three ASW patrol boats, provided by the United States in 1969, and about fourteen small (thirty-ton) gunboats—the first locally produced craft in the ROC navy—which are armed with a single forty-millimeter cannon.

A force of nine S-2A Tracker ASW aircraft enhance the ROC's antisubmarine capabilities. These aircraft, designed for operations off U.S. carriers, have about a 370-kilometer range and a nine-hour loiter time. The range is adequate for patrol in nearby waters, such as in the Taiwan Strait, but does not add to protection of its seaborne commerce very far from port.

North Korea and South Korea

Since the Korean Armistice of 1953, both North and South Korea have steadily rebuilt their armed forces with the assistance of their superpower patrons. The forces, though powerful relative to the size of the two coun-

---

60. The latest version of Gabriel has a maximum range of greater than 40 km, the Styx somewhat less than 40 km. See Richardson, "World Missiles Directory," p. 1352.

Table 2-9. Military Forces, North Korea and South Korea, 1977

North Korea	South Korea
Ground[a]	
430,000 troops	**580,000 troops**
20 infantry divisions	19 infantry divisions
12 infantry brigades	7 tank battalions
2 tank divisions	1 mechanized division
5 tank regiments	1 marine division
3 motorized infantry divisions	2 marine armored brigades
3 reconnaissance brigades	2 air defense brigades
3 antiaircraft artillery brigades	30 artillery battalions
10 antiaircraft artillery regiments	5 special forces brigades
5 airborne battalions	
3 SSM regiments	
20 artillery regiments	
1,950 tanks	**880 tanks**
Aircraft	
655 fighter/attack aircraft	**300 fighter/attack aircraft**
85 Il-28s	40 F-4D/Es
20 Su-7s	180 F-5A/Es
320 MiG-15/-17s	80 F-86Fs
120 MiG-21s	
110 MiG-19s	
Ships	
44 ships	**96 ships**
10 submarines	7 destroyers
7 frigates	9 frigates
19 submarine chasers/escorts	14 coastal escorts
18 guided-missile patrol boats	44 patrol boats
	21 landing ships

Sources: IISS, *The Military Balance, 1977–1978*, pp. 60–61; and information provided by the UN Command, Seoul, June 1978.

a. North Korea also has 40,000 paramilitary security forces and border guards and a 1–2-million-strong civilian militia. South Korea has over 1 million reserves plus about 1 million personnel in the Homeland Defense Reserve Force for rear-area security.

tries, do not represent a direct threat to other nations in the region since each is preoccupied with the prospect of conflict with the other. This section describes the armed forces of the two Koreas to illustrate the balance of indigenous forces on the peninsula (see table 2-9).

Ground Forces

The ground forces of North Korea are patterned after the Soviet army, with emphasis on large armored forces and on heavy artillery and mortar fire support.

North Korea's 1,950 tanks represent considerable offensive power, although numbers alone overstate the strength of the force since it includes many obsolescent vehicles. For example, the 350 T-34 tanks date from World War II and are inferior in firepower and armor protection to tanks of more recent design; and the PT-76 light tank, used for reconnaissance in the Soviet army, has only a small gun and light armor (because of its amphibious requirement). The rest of the tank force is composed of 900 Soviet T-54s and variations of this model: the T-55, a slightly improved version, and the T-59, a less capable Chinese version. Although the T-54 was first manufactured around 1950 and is being phased out of service in the Soviet army, it has served as the main battle tank in most Communist nations and performed adequately.

Like the Soviet army, the North Korean army incorporates a large number of artillery and mortar pieces (about 3,000 artillery and 9,000 mortar pieces). Some of the artillery is implanted in protective fortifications close to the demilitarized zone where it can shell South Korean positions while sheltered from air or artillery bombardment. In addition, North Korea has about twenty-four Soviet Frog-5/-7 surface-to-surface unguided missiles with a maximum range of fifty-five kilometers—sufficient to reach Seoul from North Korean territory.[61]

The army of the Republic of Korea (ROK) is patterned after the U.S. Army. It has developed strong combat units, which are positioned near the demilitarized zone to provide a forward defense to protect Seoul. The ROK Homeland Reserve Force is maintained elsewhere for rear-area security and antiinfiltration tasks in the event of conflict. This force can be bolstered at short notice. Finally, about 1 million reserves form a pool from which additional manpower can be drawn to replace losses in the regular forces.

South Korea plans to expand and upgrade its tank force. Its forward units now have about 880 U.S.-model M-47 and M-48 tanks. South Korea's plans include acquisition of additional M-48 tanks, which will replace most of the M-47s and increase slightly the number of tanks in the active forces. The M-48s are being fitted with a 105-millimeter gun, larger than that on North Korea's main battle tank (100-millimeter). Moreover, the accuracy and speed of the 105-millimeter gun are superior, making the M-48 the more effective tank.[62] The South has built up other

61. Richardson, "Missile Forces of the World," p. 1606.
62. See Bernard Weinraub, "The Korea Withdrawal: Some Officers are Nervous and Congress Wants to Have a Say," *New York Times,* May 30, 1977.

Table 2-10. Aircraft, North Korean and South Korean Air Forces, 1977

Type[a]	Combat radius[b] (kilometers)	Ordnance capacity[b] (tons)	Maximum speed[b] (Mach)	Year commissioned	Description
		North Korea			
Su-7	480	2.0	2.0	1956	Fighter/ground attack aircraft
Il-28	965	2.2	0.8	1950	Light bomber
MiG-21	320	1.0	2.0	1961	Interceptor
MiG-19	645	0.5	1.3	1953	Interceptor
MiG-15/17	450/580	0.5	0.9	1947–49	Fighter/ground attack aircraft
		South Korea			
F-4D/E	965	5.0	2.2+	1965–67	Fighter-bomber
F-5A/E	320/645	3.5	1.4–1.6	1963–72	Fighter-bomber
F-86F	435	1.5	0.9	1953	Fighter-bomber, interceptor

Sources: William Green and Gordon Swanborough, *The Observer's Soviet Aircraft Directory* (London: Frederick Warne, 1975), pp. 53, 143, 162, 170, 177, 203; Charles M. Gilson, "Military Aircraft of the World," *Flight International*, vol. 111 (March 5, 1977), p. 574–75.
a. Soviet-built aircraft may differ from their counterparts built in China.
b. Authors' estimates, based on sources.

antitank defenses: TOWs (tube-launched, optically tracked, wire-guided missiles), recoilless rifles, fortifications and obstacles at choke points along the approach corridors to Seoul, and air-to-ground antiarmor munitions.

Air Forces

North Korea maintains a large air force at about sixteen airfields.[63] Its capabilities are limited, however, by the age and type of equipment employed. The most modern components of the force are the MiG-21s and Su-7s. The MiG-21s, supplemented by the less capable MiG-19s, provide the North with a large interceptor force (see table 2-10 for details). The aircraft are supplemented by about 250 SA-2 surface-to-air missiles (SAMs), an early generation Soviet SAM system of limited effectiveness.

Most of North Korea's attack aircraft are obsolescent and limited in their performance. The most capable is the supersonic Su-7. The Il-28 bomber is subsonic and is vulnerable to air defenses in the south. The MiG-15 and -17 aircraft are aging and are also subsonic and vulnerable to air defenses.

63. Ralph N. Clough, *Deterrence and Defense in Korea: The Role of U.S. Forces* (Brookings Institution, 1976), p. 12.

In summary, the North Korean air defense network is dense and by sheer numbers it could make penetration of their boundaries costly in number of aircraft lost. The North's attack aircraft are obsolescent and susceptible to attrition by Southern air defenses. However, the force is large, and given its short flight time to Seoul and to the South's defensive positions, it could launch a large-scale surprise attack that would be formidable to defend against.

The ROK air force is outnumbered about three to one by the North, but its F-4D/E Phantoms are far more capable than any aircraft in the North. In addition, the F-5A/E Tigers compare favorably with the North's MiG-21s. Eighteen more F-4E and sixty F-5E/F aircraft are now on order, which will result in a modernized and slightly expanded ROK air force. Air defense is supplemented by eighty Hawk and forty Nike-Hercules SAM launchers. The aging F-86s could be used for ground strikes, although they are limited in payload and performance and vulnerable to the North's air defenses. While the F-4s could also perform this role, it would mean that fewer aircraft would be available for air defense. In short, although the ROK air force is modern and its pilots capable, these factors do not compensate for the disparity in numbers of aircraft between the North and South. The ROK air force operates from fewer fields than the North Korean air force, which makes their force more vulnerable than the North's.

Naval Forces

Much of North Korea's trade goes by overland routes to the Soviet Union and China, while all of South Korea's foreign trade must go by sea. Consequently, South Korea's commerce is an attractive target to the North, and the ROK navy must devote resources to defending that commerce. In addition, both navies have the mission of protecting their coastlines from infiltration or large-scale assaults.

The most formidable threat to ROK shipping is North Korea's submarines. They are of 1950s Soviet design, limited in range, and noisy. But range limitation is no constraint in operations against the South, and in shallow waters even noisy submarines would strain the South's ASW forces, which must rely on obsolescent equipment.

The North's surface fleet has no large modern ships. There are about nineteen ships somewhat smaller than frigates, mostly Soviet *SO*-1 class, some of which were built in North Korea. These can best be described as submarine chasers/escorts. They lack modern antiship and antiaircraft weaponry and would not be very effective in a high-threat environment. In wartime, they would probably be confined to the mission of coastal defense. Moreover, North Korea must maintain two separate fleets to defend its two coasts, since reinforcement of one or the other would involve bringing ships around the South Korean coast.

Additional coastal defense is provided by the eight *Osa*-class and ten *Komar*-class Soviet-built patrol boats. These small craft are fast (thirty-two and forty knots maximum, respectively) and are armed with the twenty-three-mile-range Styx antiship cruise missile. They would be particularly effective in opposing attempted amphibious landings. About 200 small gunboats and torpedo boats supplement the North's coastal defense force, making infiltration or amphibious landings difficult.

The North has little amphibious lift capability and could not mount a sizable invasion from the sea. It has, however, a fleet of small, fast motorboats, which could be used to infiltrate the South with terrorists and agents.

South Korea has a well-balanced fleet of surface ships. The destroyers are all former U.S. navy ships built during World War II and transferred to South Korea. They are fast (maximum speed thirty-five knots) and have a reasonable amount of firepower; each incorporates five or six 127-millimeter guns. Four of the destroyers had been modernized by the U.S. Navy and have modern ASW detection equipment, although they lack modern long-range ASW weaponry. Two more destroyers were transferred to the ROK navy in 1977; these incorporate the Asroc torpedo. In addition, some destroyers will be fitted with the U.S.-built Standard antiship missile and possibly with the Gabriel missile. This program is critical; it will extend the range and accuracy of the surface fleet's firepower to match or exceed that of the North's ships, including those armed with Styx missiles. The other surface combatants, the nine frigate-sized ships, add a substantial amount of firepower to the fleet, but their ASW capability is very limited. Some twenty S-2A/2F Tracker aircraft enhance the South's ASW capability in waters adjacent to its coast.

South Korea is modernizing its coastal patrol fleet with two new types of craft. The larger, called a multimission patrol ship (PSMM), is a 250-ton craft, capable of speeds over forty knots and of carrying four antiship missiles. It is comparable to the North's *Osa*-class patrol craft. Three PSMMs were built in the United States for the ROK navy and four more have been built in Korea. A smaller, seventy-ton coastal patrol and interdiction craft (CPIC), capable of forty-five-knot speeds and able to carry antiship missiles, has been developed by the United States for production in Korea for the ROK navy. The prototype of this CPIC was built in the United States and transferred to the ROK navy. Seven more are being built by the Koreans. Both ships will enhance the South's coastal-defense capabilities and the high speed and maneuverability of the CPIC make it especially well suited for the antiinfiltration mission.

South Korea's amphibious force is large enough to lift a force of several battalions to conduct diversionary raids during war but not large enough for more ambitious operations.

The ROK navy has no submarines. Even if it had them, the naval balance would not change greatly since North Korea depends far less than the South on sea lanes for trade or resupply of combat materiel. Submarines would, however, be useful for patrolling coastal waters against North Korean submarines.

United States

The foregoing descriptions of the armed forces of the other military actors in Northeast Asia define the military environment in which U.S. forces must operate in support of U.S. commitments in the region. These U.S. forces are described below, along with the forces that could reinforce them:[64]

Ground divisions	Aircraft	Ships
1 Second Army	390 fighters	2 aircraft carriers
1 Third Marine	14 bombers	21 destroyers, cruisers, and frigates
	66 ASW patrol	8 landing ships
	aircraft	4 submarines armed with torpedoes

Ground Forces

The Second Infantry Division is based at Camp Casey, astride the main invasion corridor from North Korea to Seoul and about forty

64. Vice Admiral George P. Steele II, U.S. Navy (Retired), "Ready Power for Peace—The U.S. Seventh Fleet," *United States Naval Institute Proceedings,* vol. 102 (January 1976), p. 27; U.S. Department of the Army, Office of Assistant Secretary of Defense, Public Affairs, "DOD Military Personnel Strength as of December 31, 1976" (April 1977); unpublished data from U.S. Department of the Navy, January 1977. One of the three regiments that forms the Third Marine Division is stationed in Hawaii.

kilometers from the demilitarized zone. About 15,000 troops are assigned to this division. Other troops associated with air defense, surveillance, ground-based nuclear weapons, and logistics support the division and the South Korean forces. In March 1977, President Carter announced plans to withdraw U.S. ground forces from Korea. Although details are still being worked out, combat units along with their support units are scheduled to leave by 1982.

In addition to the marines on Okinawa, two marine amphibious units, typically battalion landing teams, are maintained afloat in the western Pacific for quick reaction to crises. The forces afloat also include one large LPH, which can carry up to thirty-two helicopters and accommodate V/STOL aircraft; and one LPD, which also carries helicopters.

Air Forces

The air force maintains nine squadrons of F-4 aircraft in the western Pacific region. A typical deployment is outlined in table 2-11, although aircraft can be reassigned from one base to another rapidly. The marine aircraft on Honshu are organized into five fighter/attack squadrons. Additional tankers, observation aircraft, and helicopters are maintained on Okinawa.

Table 2-11. U.S. Aircraft in the Western Pacific Region, by Armed Service, 1977

Base	Number of aircraft	Type of aircraft
Air Force		
Kadena, Okinawa	72	F-4C/E
Kunsan, Korea	36	F-4C/E
Osan, Korea	24	F-4C/E
Clark, Philippines	48	F-4C/E
Guam	14	B-52
Marine Corps		
Iwakuni, Honshu	66	F-4B/J, A-4E/6A, AV-8A
Navy		
Carrier	48	F-4/14
Carrier	72	A-6/7

Sources: *Fiscal Year 1978 Authorization for Military Procurement, Research and Development, and Active Duty, Selected Reserve, and Civilian Personnel Strengths,* Hearings before the Senate Committee on Armed Services, 95 Cong. 1 sess. (GPO, 1977), pt. 6, p. 4189; unpublished data from U.S. Department of the Navy, January 1977.

Naval Forces

The U.S. presence in the western Pacific and Indian Ocean is maintained by the Seventh Fleet, which is the forward-deployed portion of the U.S. Pacific Fleet. The Seventh Fleet varies in composition as ships are rotated from the Third Fleet in the eastern Pacific, but a typical composition is shown in table 2-12.

The primary striking power of the Seventh Fleet are the task forces of the two aircraft carriers. Their primary weaponry, fighter/attack aircraft (see table 2-11), is used for fleet air defense and for strikes against other ships and shore targets. On each carrier there are also four KA-6 tanker aircraft for inflight refueling, four E-2C airborne early warning aircraft with look-down radar capability, three EA-6B aircraft for jamming enemy radar systems, and four reconnaissance aircraft. Antisubmarine warfare capability is provided by a complement of ten S-3A fixed wing aircraft and eight shorter range SH-3H helicopters.

Most of the other surface combatants are used as escorts for the carriers. The composition of any one task force will vary but typically involves about five escort ships to provide the carriers with additional ASW and air-defense capability. Supplementary ASW capability is provided by four squadrons of P-3C aircraft that operate from land bases in the western Pacific.

Six ships of the Seventh Fleet are based at Yokosuka in Japan: the carrier *Midway*, a cruiser, two destroyers, and two frigates. In addition, Sasebo, Japan, Subic Bay in the Philippines, and Guam have facilities for major ship repair and general refurbishing.

Table 2-12. Ships, U.S. Seventh Fleet, 1977

Type	Number	Displacement (tons)[a]	Primary weaponry
Aircraft carrier (CV)	2	50,000+	Fighter/attack aircraft
Cruiser (CGN, CG)	5	5,700–14,200	ASW rocket, surface-to-air missiles
Destroyer (DDG)	6	2,800–3,700	ASW rocket, surface-to-air missiles
Destroyer (DD)	3	2,400–2,800	ASW rocket, surface-to-air missiles
Frigate (FFG)	2	2,600	ASW rocket, surface-to-air missiles
Frigate (FF)	5	1,600–3,000	ASW rocket, ASW helicopter
Submarine (SSN)	4	2,600–3,800	ASW rocket, ASW torpedo
Landing ship	8	. . .	. . .

Sources: Vice Admiral George P. Steele II, U.S. Navy (Retired), "Ready Power for Peace—The U.S. Seventh Fleet," *U.S. Naval Institute, Proceedings*, vol. 102 (January 1976), p. 27; unpublished data from U.S. Department of the Navy, January 1977.

a. Dived displacement for submarines; standard displacement for surface ships.

Backup Forces

Forces in the eastern Pacific and on the west coast of the United States are equipped to reinforce quickly those deployed in the western Pacific.

Ground forces include the Twenty-fifth Army Infantry Division on Hawaii (two active brigades and one reserve brigade), the First Marine Division at Camp Pendleton, California, and one regiment of the Third Marine Division on Hawaii (its other two regiments and headquarters are on Okinawa). In addition, ten active Army Strategic Reserve divisions can be used in Asia if circumstances require them. Although five of them are more lightly equipped than front-line U.S. divisions in Europe, they are adequately equipped for a conflict in Asia.

Since air power can be deployed rapidly, it is not tied to a particular theater. The Marine Corps typically maintains about twelve fighter/attack squadrons of aircraft at Kaneohe, Hawaii; El Toro, California; and Yuma, Arizona. With the five squadrons based at Iwakuni, they form the First and Third Marine Airwings, which provide the air complement to the First and Third Marine Divisions located in the Pacific region. The U.S. Air Force maintains forty-two fighter/attack squadrons in the United States that can reinforce tactical air capabilities in any theater.

The Navy's backup force for the western Pacific is the Third Fleet, which operates east of Hawaii. It provides a training and rotation base for personnel of the Seventh Fleet and its ships routinely replace Seventh Fleet ships that need repair or maintenance (see table 2-13 for ships of the Third Fleet). Four of the six carriers assigned to the Pacific are with the Third Fleet.

Table 2-13. Ships, U.S. Third Fleet, 1977

Type	Number	Displacement (tons)[a]	Primary weaponry
Aircraft carrier (CV)	4	50,000+	Fighter/attack aircraft
Cruiser (CGN, CG)	10	5,700–14,200	ASW rocket, surface-to-air missile
Destroyer (DDG)	12	2,800–3,700	ASW rocket, surface-to-air missile
Destroyer (DD)	18	2,400–2,800	ASW rocket
Frigate (FFG)	3	2,600	ASW rocket, antiship missile
Frigate (FF)	23	1,600–3,000	ASW rocket, ASW helicopter
Submarine (SSN)	22	2,600–3,800	ASW rocket, ASW torpedo
Submarine (SS)	9	1,600–2,100	Torpedo
Landing ship	19	. . .	. . .

Source: Unpublished data from U.S. Department of the Navy, January 1977.
a. Dived displacement for submarines; standard displacement for surface ships.

Tactical Nuclear Weapons

As a backup to conventional forces, the United States maintains a stock of tactical nuclear weapons in South Korea. While details of deployments are closely guarded, the following aspects of deployment are public knowledge:

1. Nuclear warheads in South Korea number fewer than 1,000, 650 being a reasonable estimate.
2. This number is being reduced gradually.
3. The weapons are included in both army and air force armaments.
4. They are held well south of the DMZ to protect the storage sites and also to ensure that in the event of hostilities there would be time for a presidential decision regarding their employment.

The largest U.S. Army surface-to-surface weapon is the Honest John missile, which can deliver a warhead with a yield of about 100 kilotons of explosive over a range of about fifty kilometers. Most nuclear weapons in Korea can be fired from field artillery. They have a yield of one kiloton and can be fired from 155-millimeter artillery tubes. The air force also maintains nuclear munitions in Korea, and the sixty U.S. F-4s in Korea are capable of delivering them. In the event of war, however, even if the use of nuclear weapons were contemplated, only a fraction of these aircraft would be held in reserve for nuclear delivery.

Finally, the Seventh Fleet maintains some nuclear-capable attack aircraft, which could be delivered to the battlefield.

CHAPTER THREE

MILITARY PROBLEMS

In carrying out its policies toward Northeast Asia, the United States faces problems that are, at least in part, military: the Soviet naval challenge, the direct Soviet threat to Japan, danger of a new war in Korea, disagreement with Peking over Taiwan, and the possible spread of nuclear weapons.

The Soviet Naval Challenge

Although hostilities between the U.S. and Soviet navies in the Pacific are almost inconceivable—except as part of a general war, which is itself unlikely—perceptions of relative U.S. and Soviet capabilities are nevertheless of great importance. For example, if the People's Republic of China concluded the U.S. Navy was no longer supreme in the western Pacific, it would be less likely to view the United States as a useful counterweight to Soviet power and could, therefore, be less disposed to avoid a showdown with the United States over Taiwan. Of even greater potential importance, if Japan felt that the shipping lanes it depends on for essential supplies could be cut by the Soviet navy, it might question both its alignment with the United States and its policy of not building its own strong military forces. Changes in Japanese policy might follow that could prove profoundly damaging to both regional stability and U.S. interests.

Although the Soviet Far East Fleet is the poor sister of the Soviet navy, often the last to receive modern ships and aircraft, it has benefited from the modernization and expanding operations of the entire Soviet navy. Not surprisingly, most of the fleet's training exercises and equipment appear designed to prepare it to fight the U.S. Navy, with emphasis on anti-submarine warfare (ASW) and anticarrier operations. Indeed, there is only one clear instance in which the fleet practiced attack on commercial shipping, during exercise Vesna, in which a simulated convoy was "attacked" to the east of Japan.[1] Moreover, at the outset of that exercise the Soviets chose to treat the convoy as friendly, which could indicate that they were concerned with the difficult task of protecting their own growing merchant marine.

Any number of scenarios involving hostilities between the U.S. and Soviet navies in the Pacific might be imagined, but possibly the most instructive one assumes a Soviet effort to interdict Japan's supply lines. To succeed, the Soviet Far East Fleet would have to deal with the U.S. Pacific Fleet. There are several factors that would have a marked effect on the outcome of such a conflict: U.S. and Japanese success in closing the straits connecting the Sea of Japan and the Pacific Ocean; the ability of U.S. air and naval forces to impede operations from Petropavlovsk; the ability of U.S. aircraft carriers to survive the initial salvos of a conflict; and the length of time Japan could survive interdiction of its supply lines. An examination of these factors provides a context in which U.S. requirements for naval forces can be measured without tying the analysis to a specific scenario.

Closing the Straits

Geography imposes a severe disadvantage on Soviet naval operations from Vladivostok, the main base for the Soviet Far East Fleet. Ships must pass through one of the straits connecting the Sea of Japan with the Pacific Ocean. Mining these straits and/or blockading them with submarines and land-based ASW aircraft would mean that Soviet ships not already in the open ocean would be bottled up in the Sea of Japan and those outside would be forced to return elsewhere or risk being damaged or destroyed in running one of the straits.

The three major straits are the Tsushima Strait between South Korea

1. For an account of Vesna (Okean II) see the testimony of Rear Admiral B. R. Inman, U.S. Navy, director of Naval Intelligence, in *Fiscal Year 1977 Authorization for Military Procurement, Research and Development, and Active Duty, Selected Reserve and Civilian Personnel Strengths,* Hearings before the Senate Committee on Armed Services, 94 Cong. 2 sess. (Government Printing Office, 1976), pp. 5316–26.

and Japan; the Tsugaru Strait separating the Japanese islands of Honshu and Hokkaido; and the Soya (La Perouse) Strait between the northern tip of Hokkaido and the southern tip of Sakhalin. The Tsugaru Strait is bounded on both sides by Japanese territory and at one point is less than twenty-five kilometers wide and about 150 meters deep. It would be the easiest to mine. The Tsushima Strait, although bounded by friendly territory, is washed by a strong current and is 180 kilometers wide. It is difficult to mine and requires thousands of mines, all beyond the capacity of the Maritime Self Defense Force. Should conflict erupt in the near future, the United States would have to commit resources to mine the Tsushima Strait. The Soya Strait would be the most difficult to mine or to close through other means since it is bounded on the north by Soviet territory and is well within striking distance of Soviet aircraft from Sakhalin, Iterup (Eterofu), and—if the Sino-Soviet border were quiet—air bases along the Ussuri River.

But as difficult as mining could be, the strategic advantage would still lie with the West. Only a few heavy-lift aircraft need successfully drop mines, whereas Soviet interception of the mining operation would have to be 100 percent successful. Even a thin seeding of the straits would establish a probability of submarine kill, making it risky for valuable submarines to pass through the field. The Captor mine will reduce the number of drops necessary to attain a given probability of kill and thereby will reduce the length of time the seeding aircraft are exposed to Soviet fire.[2]

Naturally, the earlier the closing, the more effective it is. Since steady deployment of the Soviet fleet outside of the area is low, it could be crippled by closure of the straits at the outset of a conflict. If the Soviets were contemplating military action, they could of course increase deployment elsewhere. But this would signal Soviet intentions, allowing the United States time to enhance the readiness of the U.S. fleet and so avoid being stung by a large preemptive strike.

How quickly the straits could be closed rests largely on Japanese co-operation. The airfields of its Air Self Defense Force are good staging areas for mining operations and also for the air cover for the mining craft. Though the mining could be done by submarines, it would be time-consuming and would expose this valuable and limited resource to detection and destruction early in the campaign.

2. The Captor system senses the acoustic signature of a passing submarine and launches a Mark-48 torpedo, which homes on the submarine. Captor has just recently begun to enter the U.S. Navy inventory.

Closing Off Petropavlovsk

Because of the vulnerability of the straits, the Soviet Union developed naval facilities at Petropavlovsk, on the Kamchatka peninsula, to establish a base with access to the Pacific. There are, in addition, four naval air stations nearby.

Although Petropavlovsk has no choke point, the twenty-six nuclear-powered attack submarines assigned to the U.S. Pacific Fleet could still impede its operations. In addition, the port has no adequate rail or road links with central or western USSR, so most supplies are brought by surface ship from Vladivostok. Thus closing the straits would complicate logistical support of Petropavlovsk. Furthermore, the supply ships are vulnerable to air attack, and convoying and protecting them would drain resources from other operations. Harassment of the Soviet supply effort would be increasingly effective as time passed, and in protracted hostilities, time would be on the side of the United States and Japan.

Keeping U.S. Carriers Afloat

U.S. naval power in the western Pacific is concentrated in the task force of two aircraft carriers maintained in the area. In the event of a global naval conflict, strike elements of the U.S. Third Fleet in the eastern Pacific are slated to redeploy to the Atlantic, leaving a limited reserve from which the Seventh Fleet could replenish its losses. The loss of even one of the carriers would cripple U.S. capabilities in the region. The most devastating development would be a Soviet strike that neutralized the carriers at the outset of hostilities.

The Soviet navy has two anticarrier weapons: the torpedo and the anti-ship cruise missile. The submarine-launched torpedo is not a new threat and the U.S. Navy (and other navies in the region) have adjusted to it. Although the Soviet navy has replaced short-range, conventionally powered submarines with long-range, nuclear-powered submarines, the antisubmarine capabilities of the U.S. Navy have improved too, probably equally. Antisubmarine defenses to protect the carrier (in contrast to search-and-track operations to monitor submarine movements over broad expanses of the ocean) are provided by S-3A Viking ASW aircraft, SH-3 Sea King ASW helicopters, and surface escorts.

If the resources were available, a U.S. nuclear-powered attack submarine could be coordinated with the carrier group to provide another

dimension of protection. In recent years, Vikings have been equipped with improved acoustic processors and sonobuoys. Introduction of LAMPS and development of tactical towed-array sonar will enhance the ASW capacity of the surface escorts.[3] Finally, should a submarine penetrate the screen and launch a torpedo that scores a hit, the carrier may not sink, because its double hull construction and other features allow it to withstand at least one hit.

The antiship cruise missile is a far more serious threat. Soviet SS-N-2 Styx missiles launched from an Egyptian patrol boat sank the Israeli destroyer *Eilat* in 1967, giving a preview of the potential of this weapon in naval warfare. During the 1971 Indo-Pakistani conflict, Indian patrol boats armed with Styx missiles sank one Pakistani destroyer and seriously damaged another, confirming the efficacy of the system against surface ships. And in the 1973 Middle East war, the Israeli navy scored notable success with its missile-equipped ships. How effective the cruise missile would be against an aircraft carrier, which is many times larger than a destroyer, is not known. It would be a coincidence if a single cruise missile (unless it is armed with a nuclear warhead) disabled a carrier or even seriously degraded its effectiveness. Several hits, however, would cripple a carrier enough to force it to return to base for repairs.

Loss of the carrier air wing would render defense of ships against an air strike a far more difficult task, depleting assets for antiship and antisubmarine operations and, of course, for shore strikes. However, if U.S. airforce and marine bases in Japan had facilities for U.S. carrier aircraft, they could still be used even if a carrier were in port or disabled. The Congressional Budget Office estimated that providing such facilities in Europe would require a one-time outlay of $80 million and maintenance costs of $3 million annually (figures in fiscal year 1977 dollars).[4] Naturally, access to bases in Japan would be critical also for land-based aircraft, if they were given the disabled carrier's tasks.

The Soviet naval strategy is to employ numerous cruise missiles in a brief coordinated surprise strike against hostile ships.[5] During military

3. LAMPS (light airborne multipurpose system) is an SH-2 Seasprite helicopter equipped with modern antisubmarine systems, including dipping sonar, and deploys from a surface ship.

4. Congressional Budget Office, *Planning U.S. General Purpose Forces: The Tactical Air Forces* (GPO: 1977), p. 41.

5. For a discussion of Soviet naval strategy, see Admiral S. G. Gorshkov, "The Development of the Art of Naval Warfare," *Proceedings of the U.S. Naval Institute*, vol. 101 (June 1975), pp. 55–63.

exercise Okean 75, the Soviet Union simulated launches of cruise missiles from aircraft, surface ships, and submarines against U.S. carrier groups.

It is unlikely that a carrier could avoid being hit in such a preemptive salvo. In a recent study, the National Security Council reached a preliminary conclusion that in the face of such an attack, if the carrier force had to fall back on its final point defenses, "present U.S. surface-to-air missile systems [would not be] effective against the newer generation Soviet antiship missiles. The time from detection until target engagement is excessive, and coordination among missile batteries on different ships in the task force is poor."[6]

The capabilities of the Soviet Far East Fleet to mount such an attack are less formidable than those of the fleets in the western Soviet Union. Their Tu-16 aircraft have the range to strike ships in the seas east and south of Japan, but to do so they must fly over Japanese territory where they are vulnerable to attack from land-based aircraft (since they are subsonic and not capable of extended low altitude flight). Should the initial salvo fail, Soviet surface ships would be extremely vulnerable to counterattack from carrier-based or land-based aircraft. The fleet's nuclear-powered guided missile submarines (four *Charlies* and fourteen *Echo II*s) would be difficult to defend against, particularly *Charlies,* which can launch while submerged.

In summary, if U.S. carrier groups can avoid exposure to a surprise initial salvo, their chances of surviving for an extended period are good; it is doubtful that Soviet surface ships could operate long in the vicinity of carrier-based or land-based air coverage. Submarines would remain a problem. If they were locked out of Vladivostok and if operations at Petropavlovsk were hampered, however, the size and effectiveness of the force would decrease with time as U.S. antisubmarine operations continued.

Developments that could improve carrier survivability include the Phoenix air-to-air missile (deployed on F-14 Tomcat fighters), which can intercept missile-armed aircraft or the cruise missiles themselves. The AEGIS surface-to-air weapons system is intended to help defend against a salvo of antiship cruise missiles. It is designed to track a large number of incoming targets simultaneously and direct a counterlaunch of defensive missiles. On the other hand, deployment in numbers of the new

6. National Security Council study of U.S. maritime strategy, as quoted in "The Three Major Threats to U.S. Fleet," *Defense/Space Business Daily,* October 15, 1976.

Soviet Tu-26 Backfire bomber, which can carry two antiship cruise missiles, would complicate the problem of carrier survivability. The Tu-26 has a much greater combat radius than the principal medium-range bomber now in use, the Tu-16 Badger. The Tu-26 can fly at supersonic speeds and at low altitudes, making detection, tracking, and interception difficult. Its disadvantage in attacking carriers is loss of range when flying either over Japan (because it would have to penetrate at low altitude) or north of Hokkaido.

Keeping the Japanese Economy Going

The length of time Japan's economy could withstand sharply reduced imports would have a great effect on Japan's security in time of crisis—whether the crisis were a USSR threat of a naval blockade, a U.S.-Soviet conflict in which Japan attempted to minimize its involvement, or a U.S.-Soviet conflict in which Japan participated fully. The efficacy of a threat of a blockade would depend, in part, on the capacity Japan felt it had to withstand a sharp drop in imports. The threat most difficult to counter would be from the submarines of the Soviet Far East Fleet. Antisubmarine warfare is a tedious process; but the longer the Japanese economy functions, the greater the probability of success in clearing the sea-lanes.

One recent analysis isolated three economic measures that would reduce Japan's heavy import requirements and thus increase Japan's capacity to function despite the interdiction of its sea-going trade: (1) *Reduce personal consumption.* Although unpopular, this is a normal wartime measure. (2) *Suspend production of export goods.* This requires substantial foreign exchange reserves and possibly a healthy credit rating abroad. (3) *Increase stocks of petroleum and raw materials.* The present goal is petroleum stocks enough for ninety days of peacetime consumption.[7] Together, these measures could reduce ship arrivals from a peacetime level of about 2,000 a month to 250 or less (depending on the amount of stockpiling, particularly of petroleum, which accounts for about 50 percent by weight of Japan's imports).[8]

7. David Shilling, "A Reassessment of Japan's Naval Defense Needs," *Asian Survey,* vol. 16 (March 1976), pp. 221, 223–24. The Japanese government hopes to achieve the goal of increased petroleum stocks by the end of 1979. See Japan Ministry of Foreign Affairs, Public Information Bureau, *Information Bulletin* (April 1, 1977), p. 6.
8. Shilling, "Japan's Naval Defense Needs," pp. 223–24.

In addition, by diversifying its sources of imports, Japan could lessen the difficulty of protecting its essential shipping. The shortest of Japan's major trade lanes, and the most easily defended, is that originating in Indonesia and extending about 3,000 kilometers north to Japan. Assuming austere consumption, about a third of Japan's petroleum could be supplied by this route, permitting a slower drawdown of stockpiles and increasing the cushion by another third.[9] Recent trade agreements with the PRC may provide yet another, shorter, major import route.

The Backfire bomber could increase convoying problems. Although the Maritime Self Defense Force has only limited air defense capability, convoys through the Philippine Sea could sail north close to the Philippines and Okinawa, thus staying in range of U.S. and Japanese land-based air cover.[10] Radar with low-altitude detection capability would be needed to defend against Backfire's low-altitude approach. If Air Self Defense Force plans to purchase E-2C Hawkeye warning and control aircraft come to fruition, Japan would have some capability in this area. However, only the U.S. Airborne Warning and Control System (AWACS) could provide adequate detection over a broad area of low-altitude attack.

The Direct Soviet Threat to Japan

Although the threat of direct Soviet attack on Japan's home islands is remote, the heavy concentration of industry in the narrow belt from Tokyo to Osaka is an attractive target for air attack.

The Japan Air Self Defense Force is responsible for monitoring and protecting Japan's air space. Japan's air-defense radar system, base air-defense ground environment (BADGE), with twenty-eight radar sites, continuously scans the air space around Japan. The units check aircraft approaching Japanese air space, and interceptors from the nearest field scramble to investigate any aircraft not obviously friendly. Five air defense missile groups, operating Nike and Hawk missile units, back up the interceptors.

The best Japan could hope to do in the face of a Soviet air attack would be to make that attack very costly. In a massive bombing attack, some Soviet bombers would penetrate Japan's defenses. However, the Tu-16s, the bulk of the Soviet Long Range Aviation bombers in the Far East,

9. Ibid., pp. 225, 227.
10. U.S. aircraft might also be able to use airfields on Taiwan.

are vulnerable to detection and tracking by the BADGE radar units and to interception by Japanese fighter aircraft (particularly if they are augmented by U.S. fighter squadrons from Okinawa, the Philippines, and Korea).

But of concern for the future is the introduction of the Backfire bomber. The Backfire can fly at low altitudes and therefore might avoid detection and tracking by the BADGE radar system. Unless it can detect and track the invader, Japan's ability to intercept the invader is weak. The Air Self Defense Force's E-2C Hawkeye airborne warning and control aircraft will give at least some ability, albeit thin, to monitor an aircraft approaching at low altitude and vector the interceptors to the proper vicinity. In addition, Japan has contracted for 100 F-15 Eagle fighter aircraft to begin production in 1980. The F-15 has the speed (Mach 2.5+), maneuverability, and radar adequate to counter the Backfire as well as the older Soviet bombers.

There seems to be little motivation for a Soviet ground invasion and occupation of Japan's home islands. Japan is most vulnerable to attacks on its shipping and strikes from the air, and the USSR's relatively modest amphibious capability in the Far East makes land invasion only a remote possibility.

Speculation on the role of the Soviet Union's small naval infantry contingent in the Far East has centered on seizure of the Japanese shore of the Soya Strait to impede U.S. and Japanese attempts to mine the straits. But even this limited objective would be difficult to achieve. The equipment of the Ground Self Defense Force on Hokkaido has been modernized, adding mobility, armor, and firepower. If this force acquires precision-guided antiarmor weapons, a landing would be even more unattractive from the Soviet point of view.

The Danger of War in Korea

A conflict in Korea would impose a great strain on the United States' relatively peaceful accommodation with China and the Soviet Union. For Japan, it could stir national feelings of insecurity, sharpen domestic political differences, and precipitate an examination of its present lightly armed, nonnuclear status.

The strategy for preserving peace in Korea has been to maintain a stable balance of power on the peninsula: making sure that the U.S. and Korean forces in the South could defend against attack, while at the same time not building up the South's offensive power to the point where it would be tempted to march North. U.S. forces have been an important part of this balance since the armistice ended the Korean War in July 1953. At that time, the United States, judging that the army of the Republic of Korea (ROK) could not by itself provide for the defense of the country, kept two U.S. army infantry divisions on the peninsula. Not until 1971 was any major change made in this deployment. In that year the Seventh Division and its support units were withdrawn, reflecting U.S. satisfaction with the capability of ROK ground forces and the performance of the ROK economy. In March 1977, President Carter, citing these same factors, announced his intention of removing the remaining U.S. ground combat forces, the U.S. Army Second Division. There is disagreement over whether the withdrawal of the Second Division is a prudent risk, as the administration maintains, or whether it will shift the military balance and "lead to war," a position taken by Major General John K. Singlaub, former chief of staff of U.S. Forces, Korea.[11]

A conflict in Korea would be decided primarily by the effectiveness of the opposing ground forces. The only attractive naval target for North Korea is the port of Pusan, through which most of Korea's materiel would be shipped during wartime. The North, with overland links to both China and the Soviet Union, is not dependent on shipping at all. Although air strikes on communication centers, air defense radar sites, and airfields could give one side a meaningful advantage, in the Korean War U.S. air superiority over nearly the entire peninsula was by no means decisive.

During the Korean War, the rapid initial advance of the North Korean army was aided by its force of T-34 tanks, which penetrated the South's defenses, enabling the infantry to exploit the breach. But this tactic is effective only as long as the defending forces have no antiarmor munitions. And because the terrain is rugged and armor must be restricted to corridors, the amount of armor an attacker could usefully employ in battle at any one time is limited. Massed, roadbound armor is particularly vulnerable to fire from dug-in defensive positions and strikes from the air. Barring dramatic imbalances in armor and antiarmor capability, armored operations in Korea are not likely to be decisive, as they were in Europe in World War II. The infantry was crucial in the later stages of the Korean War and is likely to be equally important in another war.

11. *Washington Post,* May 19, 1977.

Geography

Because the ridges of mountains generally run north-south, both attacker and defender are forced to operate in corridors. Should the attacking forces be concentrated where defensive forces are weak, timely reinforcement by the defender would be difficult. The Taebaek mountain range is a particularly imposing barrier, isolating ROK forces on the east coast from the bulk of the forces in the west. Terrain also limits the usefulness of simple communications equipment, since communication across mountain ranges demands sophisticated equipment.

Equally significant in its effect on the South's defense strategy is the location of Seoul, only forty kilometers from the demilitarized zone (DMZ). The North Korean capital, Pyongyang, on the other hand, is about 150 kilometers from the DMZ. Seoul has a population of 6.8 million, more than 20 percent of the total population of South Korea, with much of the nation's industry in or around it. Once driven out of Seoul, ROK forces would find it difficult to regroup and to retake the city. A successful defense of the South must be a forward defense. Since Seoul would be the obvious prize of a North Korean offensive, the South concentrates its defensive efforts along the corridors leading from the DMZ to the city. The short distance from the DMZ to the city does not allow for a defense in depth and puts a high premium on good surveillance and intelligence—to avoid a surprise attack—and troops that are rigorously trained, highly motivated, and kept at the ready. In the early stages of the Korean War, ROK troops were poorly trained and equipped and failed to resist North Korean attacks, even those not supported by armor. In general, South Korean troops are now highly motivated, and, discontent with the policies of the Park Chung Hee government notwithstanding, the citizenry is overwhelmingly anti-Communist and could be expected to resist stiffly an attack by the North.

A forward defense, in which the defender cannot afford to yield a great deal of territory, demands heavy artillery and mortar bombardment and close air support. Moreover, a heavy barrage of indirect fire spends a lot of munitions in the first days of a conflict, and ROK conventional munitions in place may be inadequate. Also, the logistics network for moving supplies from the port of Pusan or airfields in the South to the combat area is thin, and since they would come primarily from the United States, would require weeks of transit time. Adequate stocks of conventional ammunition in the theater would go a long way to enhancing South Korea's defense capability.

In a blitzkrieg invasion of Seoul, North Korean armor would be forced to use the same invasion corridors it used in the Korean War: the two corridors that merge into one at Uijongbu, sixteen kilometers north of Seoul; and a corridor further west—near Panmunjon and passing through Musan. At key choke points along these corridors are manned fortifications and concrete impediments that can be dropped onto the roadway by blowing up their supports. Invading tanks would be particularly vulnerable at these points, since they would be exposed to fire from defenders who are well dug in and therefore difficult to suppress with artillery fire. While the roadblocks would not prevent an armored advance, they would slow it, making it vulnerable to air or ground fire.

South Korea recently purchased several hundred TOW antitank missiles.[12] Test firings and combat use in the 1973 Middle East war indicate that each TOW launch has a high probability of destroying an armored vehicle. The system gives infantry a low-cost antitank capability and further complicates a North Korean blitzkrieg strategy. Finally, the ROK air force has about thirty-seven F-4 aircraft capable of ground strikes against armored targets.

In summary, the limitations imposed by terrain combined with the South's antiarmor weapons are serious obstacles to a blitzkrieg invasion from the North. The experience of 1950, when North Korean tanks drove down the peninsula unopposed, is not likely to be repeated. Still, problems remain in the ROK's defenses.

One problem inherent in the South's adoption of a defensive posture is that the North can choose the place of attack and the South has limited capability to reinforce it. Troops and supplies have to be moved by truck, and driving east or west below the DMZ is tortuous. The South's helicopter airlift capacity is insufficient to provide meaningful resupply or reinforcement. Reinforcement of defenses on the east coast would be most difficult, although since the area is thinly populated and has few military targets, ROK forces could trade space for time; no such luxury is available in the invasion corridors leading to Seoul.

Adequacy of Force Structures

GROUND. Most of the 430,000-man North Korean army is stationed near the DMZ, with the greatest concentration in the west at the head of the two principal invasion corridors to Seoul. The North Korean army,

---

12. TOW is an acronym for tube-launched, optically tracked, wire-guided.

like the Soviet army after which it is patterned, is prepared for a short, intense war. It is trained and equipped for a blitzkrieg-style attack, spearheaded by a massed tank thrust and supported by heavy artillery and mortar bombardment. Against this threat, the ROK maintains an active ground force of about 560,000 men, organized into twenty divisions. The troops are concentrated near the DMZ, except for two divisions of marines, one deployed on an island off the northwest corner of South Korea and one deployed to the west of Seoul along a rather unlikely invasion route.

Although surveillance is necessary to prepare an appropriate defense, the South's reconnaissance capabilities are rudimentary and only U.S. army installations can provide the necessary intelligence on a timely and reliable basis. Similarly, the ROK forces possess only basic communications equipment and must rely on the more sophisticated equipment operated by the U.S. Army for theater-wide command and control. Another shortcoming of the ROK forces is a thin logistics infrastructure. As South Korea rebuilt its armed forces following the Korean War, primary emphasis was put on the combat units. The army and marines were expanded to twenty-one active divisions, but a sufficient number of support units were not established concurrently. This would have little effect on the tide of battle during the opening days of the war, but it would limit the staying power of the ROK forces. War plans include mobilization of commercial trucking to haul materiel from Pusan to the front, but how rapidly this resource could be brought into efficient operation is uncertain. Moreover, the ROK forces are also thin in their capacity to repair and maintain their equipment during wartime.

AIR. The North Korean air force resembles the Soviet air force of ten to twenty years ago: most of its aircraft are limited in range and ordnance-carrying capability and are best suited for air defense. Much of its equipment is obsolescent. It is very doubtful that the North could mount a serious strike on targets deep in the South, such as Pusan or Taegu. The bomber force, made up of subsonic Il-28s, is vulnerable to interception, and even if it survived, its modest ordnance capability would yield a low payoff for a large risk. There are, however, high-priority targets near the DMZ. Communications and surveillance centers and air-defense radar sites are generally on high ground for best transmission and reception and are near North Korea's forward airfields, leaving too short a scramble time for defending aircraft. Defense of these sites is left to the Hawk surface-to-air missiles, operated by the U.S. Army. Doubtless some of the sites would be damaged and would lose some command and control and surveillance capability; but the North would lose aircraft. Missile defenses against aerial attacks on bridges across the Han River could be supplemented by interceptors, so it is unlikely that enough of the bridges could be kept out of operation long enough to isolate Seoul from the rest of the country.

As the conflict progressed, the South's higher quality aircraft would probably tip the battle toward the South. Many of North Korea's aircraft are obsolescent. Their performance capability is limited and, further, they may not hold up under the demands of the high sortie rates typical of combat. Even so, if the North massed its aircraft in attacks at the outset of a conflict, the South's quantitative handicap would not be offset by its qualitative advantages. In addition, without support from the U.S. Air Force, the ROK air force probably would be unable to spare the aircraft needed for a meaningful number of strikes against targets in the North. If it struck without air superiority, the strikes would be costly in aircraft lost. And if the Soviet Union were to provide North Korea with its latest surface-to-air missiles and guns, aircraft losses would be yet more extreme.

SEA. The navies of North Korea and South Korea could make invasion by sea very costly to both countries. North Korea is at a slight tactical disadvantage, since it must maintain a navy on each coast, whereas the South can move naval forces through friendly waters from one coast to the other. But South Korea, with no land links to its allies, is in effect an island and depends on seaborne commerce for replacement of war materiel. The North's submarines probably cannot be countered by the ROK destroyers and patrol craft, but aid from the U.S. Seventh Fleet would probably be sufficient to maintain the necessary flow of shipping.

The Future

The future U.S. force posture in Korea depends on the extent the two Koreas upgrade their armed forces. The Republic of Korea began a five-year force improvement plan to follow its force modernization plan. Unlike the modernization plan, the $4.5+ billion improvement plan is funded entirely by Korea; the only U.S. assistance is in military sales credits.[13] The air force will be affected the most: an additional 18 F-4Es

13. Hubert H. Humphrey and John Glenn, *U.S. Troop Withdrawal from the Republic of Korea,* a report to the Senate Committee on Foreign Relations, 95 Cong. 2 sess. (GPO, 1978), pp. 44–45.

were ordered; 126 F-5E fighter-bombers and 9 F-5F trainers are gradually replacing the currently deployed F-5As and F-5Bs. The South Korean government has requested the F-16 (although no decision has been reached), and an order for the A-10A appears imminent.[14] In addition, the government is modernizing its inventory of tanks and has completed an agreement with Hughes Helicopters to coproduce 100 helicopters (500M-D Defenders), some of which will carry the TOW antitank missile.[15] (This promises to be the beginning of a modest aviation industry.) The ROK navy has ordered 120 Harpoon antiship cruise missiles.

Success of the improvement plan is contingent on continued expansion of the ROK economy. The plan is predicated on an 8 percent yearly rate of real growth in the South Korean gross national product. And barring a sharp increase in the price of petroleum or a serious recession in the industrialized world, this rate should be realized. In the past decade the growth rate has exceeded 8 percent a year; in 1976 it was 15 percent, and the estimate for 1977 is 10 percent.[16] Although the improvement plan would impose a heavy balance-of-payments burden, the South's successes in diversifying its exports and markets promise to ameliorate that burden. Moreover, South Korea has attracted foreign investment, which has led to an influx of technology and industrial expertise. The South is laying a foundation for heavy industry and will eventually be capable of manufacturing significant portions of its military equipment.

Less information is available about North Korean plans to expand or modernize their forces. Much North Korean equipment is obsolescent and badly in need of replacement, the T-34 tanks and MiG-15 aircraft being prime examples. For air defense needs, the North might follow the example of Egypt and Syria, which procured large numbers of Soviet-made mobile ground-based antiaircraft systems (SA-6, SA-7, and ZSU-23-4). Experience in the 1973 war in the Middle East indicates such systems would make ground strikes against advancing North Korean armor extremely difficult.

But any broad modernization of the North Korean armed forces would be extremely expensive and difficult for North Korea's economy to finance. Its recent attempts to attract foreign investment to expand its

14. Barry Wheeler, "World's Air Forces 1978," *Flight International*, vol. 114 (July 8, 1978), p. 130.

15. Ibid.

16. Humphrey and Glenn, *U.S. Troop Withdrawal*, pp. 73–74.

Table 3-1. Indicators of Economic Size and Military Spending, North Korea and South Korea, 1976

Indicator	North Korea	South Korea
Population (millions)	17.0	36.9
Armed forces per 1,000 population	29.4	16.5
Gross national product (millions of U.S. dollars)	10,471	22,690
Military spending (millions of U.S. dollars)	1,000	1,380
Military spending as percent of gross national product	9.6	6.1

Source: U.S. Arms Control and Disarmament Agency, *World Military Expenditures and Arms Transfers, 1967–1976* (Washington: ACDA, 1978), pp. 50, 93.

economy have met with disaster. Indeed, by the end of 1976, Pyongyang had apparently defaulted on about $62 million in obligations to Japanese investors,[17] drying up sources of foreign investment. In short, if North Korea is to undertake a meaningful modernization of its armed forces, it will require aid from China or the Soviet Union. China is operating with increasingly obsolescent equipment, itself, and is hardly a fruitful source for modern military technology. The Soviet Union has the wherewithal to modernize North Korea's forces, but items from its most recent generation of military equipment have yet to appear in North Korea's forces.

Overall, time seems to be on the side of South Korea. It has already overtaken the North's head start in industrial capacity, which dates from Japanese colonial days. Barring severe political turmoil or an extended economic recession in the industrialized world, the South's lead should widen both in manufacturing and agricultural capability. Table 3-1 shows relative sizes of the two economies and the resources allocated to defense.

Two points are obvious from the table: the South has over twice the population from which to draft troops and more than double the gross national product to draw on to equip them. It should be noted that military expenditures do not necessarily result in proportionate increases to military capabilities. For example, manpower costs in the North are presumed to be less than in the South. On the other hand, the South's force improvement plan includes acquisition of U.S. surplus tanks—high-quality equipment at rather low cost.

17. B. C. Koh, "North Korea 1976: Under Stress," *Asian Survey*, vol. 17 (January 1977), p. 67.

U.S. Military Forces in South Korea

In early 1978, almost 41,000 U.S. military personnel were in Korea.[18] The largest single unit—the U.S. Armed Second Infantry Division—is located primarily at Camp Casey, about 30 kilometers from the demilitarized zone along the most direct invasion route to Seoul. Its 15,000 men do not greatly enhance the substantial ROK ground combat forces. Although the division is in the Eighth Army Reserve, one battalion is located forward to provide security for United Nations personnel at Panmunjon. Should fighting break out with little or no warning, this battalion would very likely be involved in the very early stages. And if the ROK defenses did not hold, the battle could reach the main portion of the Second Division in one or two days.[19]

The Second Division operates under the direction of a unique command structure. The United Nations Command is composed almost entirely of ROK troops plus token forces from a handful of other nations but is commanded by a U.S. army general. The Second Division and twelve ROK divisions compose the I Corps Group, a force deployed along critical areas between the DMZ and Seoul. The commander of I Corps Group is a U.S. lieutenant general, who thus exercises operational control over the very core of the ROK army. Because of the key U.S. positions in the command structure, the United States has been able to insure that the ROK would not overreact to border incidents.

The Nineteenth Support Brigade and the Second Transportation Company support the Second Division logistically. There is little room for reduction of the 3,700 U.S. soldiers in these units as long as the Second Division remains in Korea.

The Thirty-eighth Air Defense Artillery Brigade operates air defense systems, the most important of which is the Hawk surface-to-air missile, which provides point defense against air attack. This is particularly crucial in the forward areas where flight time from North Korean airfields is too short for interceptor aircraft to respond from friendly airfields. In-

---

18. Information on location and number of U.S. forces stationed in Korea from Humphrey and Glenn, *U.S. Troop Withdrawal,* pp. 35–42; and U.S. Department of Defense, Office of the Secretary of Defense, "DOD Military Personnel Strengths by Regional Area and by Country," March 28, 1978.

19. The small U.S. force assigned to the Joint Security Area would be involved almost immediately. This force of about 100 men is not part of the Second Division.

deed, the Hawk is the first line of air defense against preemptive strikes on forward communications, surveillance, and air defense radar, which are generally on high ground and particularly vulnerable. Plans to train ROK nationals to operate the Hawk are formulated, and the transfer of responsibility for the system is scheduled for 1982.

The First Signal Brigade, about 3,000 men, maintains the communications and surveillance networks. The communications equipment is sophisticated and can be maintained and operated only by U.S. personnel. There will be no ROK nationals with training adequate to operate the installations in the near future. If communications depended on the equipment ROK nationals could operate, the commander's ability to communicate, and hence exercise command and control throughout the theater, would be sharply curtailed. Moreover, it is the surveillance capability of this group on which the UN Command depends for early warning of a buildup in the North. The proximity of Seoul to the DMZ makes an early warning capability vital.

The Fourth Missile Brigade operates surface-to-surface missiles, including nuclear capable delivery systems. Until recently these included the Honest John and Sergeant systems, but the U.S. Army announced in April 1977 that the latter system is to be withdrawn.

The U.S. Air Force maintains the equivalent of a full air wing of F-4C/E tactical fighter aircraft, split between the Eighth Tactical Fighter Wing at Osan, located forward near Seoul, and the Fifty-first Composite Tactical Wing at Kunsan, about 160 kilometers further south. These units can be reinforced rapidly by the Nineteenth Tactical Fighter Wing stationed at Kadena Air Force Base in Okinawa and by the First U.S. Marine Air Wing at Iwakuni, Japan (see table 2-11). Carrier aircraft can be brought into the conflict as well. These combined forces, together with the ROK air force, would be more than an adequate match for North Korea's air force. Nevertheless, coping with a massive preemptive air strike by the North would remain a difficult problem.

There are also U.S. units in Japan, maintaining facilities that would support military operations in Korea. During the Korean War the bases served as safe areas for short-term storage of materiel destined for Korea, as holding points for personnel being moved to and from the front, and as staging areas for bombing raids.

Two trends have reduced their importance to the defense of Korea. First, since the Korean War, South Korean bases have improved greatly, and facilities now exist both at airfields (notably those near Kunsan, Osan, Taegu, and Seoul) and at ports (Pusan and, to a lesser extent, Inchon) to handle much of the materiel arriving from the United States, which earlier might have come through Japan. Second, the range and capacity of the U.S. air force military cargo fleet has been enhanced greatly since the Korean War. Direct airlift from the United States to Korea is now the most efficient means of supplying forces there. These two trends have not eliminated entirely the utility of the Japanese bases in the event of a Korean conflict. The Korean base structure is only marginally adequate to handle a major supply effort, and it could be a decade before they are adequate unless the United States assists. In any event, U.S. air bases (particularly at Kadena, Okinawa) and naval bases (particularly at Yokosuka) would continue to be valuable staging areas for U.S. air and naval support of South Korea.

The U.S. navy presence in Korea is largely to advise the ROK navy and to coordinate its operations with the Seventh Fleet. But in wartime, the Seventh Fleet would have to aid the ROK navy, particularly by preventing the North's submarine force from interdicting vital shipping, to ensure a flow of war materiel and other imported supplies into Pusan.

The Taiwan Problem

The Chinese Communist leaders show no signs of seeking an early military solution to the Taiwan problem, but at the same time they refuse to declare they will not use force in making good their claim to legal sovereignty over the island. If the Chinese Communists one day do decide to try to gain control of Taiwan by military means, they can choose among several options, all of which involve serious problems for them.

Nuclear Attack on Taiwan

First, Peking could demand that the Chinese Nationalists surrender Taiwan or suffer a nuclear attack. Such a threat might trigger a counter-ultimatum by the United States and certainly would jeopardize Peking's relations with other countries. Furthermore, any threat of nuclear attack might set a precedent for the Soviet Union in its quarrel with China. And what if the Nationalists did not capitulate? Could Peking actually carry through its threat, especially since it would result in the deaths of large numbers of its own people? The answer is almost certainly negative. The possibility is therefore most unlikely.

Conventional Attack on Taiwan

Second, Peking might consider an all-out conventional offensive against Taiwan—to try to take the island by storm. This, too, would bring political penalties, though probably less than those following a threatened or actual use of nuclear weapons. U.S. intervention to keep the attack from succeeding would be a strong possibility, but even if Peking believed this unlikely, it would not find an all-out attack against Taiwan an attractive military enterprise.

Over a period of years, Peking could no doubt amass the amphibious fleet needed to seize a beachhead on Taiwan's west coast. The People's Liberation Army has had little amphibious experience, however, except for river crossings. The landing on Quemoy late in the civil war ended in total disaster. As risky as crossing a hundred miles and more of stormy water would be, landing on a heavily defended shore without strong support from naval gunfire would be even more so. And since the PRC air force consists principally of short-range aircraft best suited for air defense, it cannot be relied on to overcome coastal defenses.

Attrition might give Peking the air superiority over the Taiwan Strait that is essential to the success of a landing, since its air force is over seventeen times larger than the Nationalists'.[20] The cost, however, would be heavy, because the Nationalists have more modern planes and defend Taiwan with surface-to-air missiles.

If a successful landing were made on Taiwan, the landing force might be destroyed by the strong Nationalist ground forces before it could be reinforced from across the Taiwan Strait. And if the United States intervened to block reinforcement, failure of the amphibious attack would be virtually certain. But even if the United States stood aside—which Peking could not count on—the outcome would not be predictable. Only the high cost of the effort would be certain.

---

20. This ratio is somewhat misleading, since Peking would not strip its defenses along the Soviet border in order to commit all of its air assets to the attack on Taiwan. Moreover, as long as pilots were available, the Nationalists might be able to make up losses of aircraft by obtaining replacements from the United States.

Attack on Offshore Islands

A third possibility, politically and militarily less hazardous, is to try to seize one or more of the offshore islands held by Nationalist forces.[21] Such an effort would appear militarily more feasible than an all-out attack on Taiwan. The risk of U.S. military intervention is much lower, because the formal U.S. security commitment to the Republic of China is limited to Taiwan and the Pescadores.

Quemoy is the most likely objective, because it lies closest to the mainland and because loss of its large garrison (60,000 men or about a sixth of the Nationalist ground forces) would be a more severe blow to morale on Taiwan than would loss of the much smaller garrisons on other islands. Peking would probably calculate that they could force surrender by cutting off supplies from Taiwan through combined naval and air power and artillery fire from the mainland. Nationalist prospects of reopening supply lines to Quemoy would be poor, even if all available air and naval forces were committed to the task.[22] Taipei would in fact probably refrain from an all-out effort to resupply Quemoy, in order to husband its air and naval assets to meet a possible attack on Taiwan. From a strictly military point of view, the surrender of Quemoy would therefore be only a matter of time.

The amount of time, however, could be long. The Nationalists store large stocks of supplies in underground areas on Quemoy. If morale held, the garrison could probably hold out for many months. The prolonged siege would bring the plight of the garrison to world attention, and political pressure could build against Peking, especially from Washington and Tokyo. Peking could of course try to end the affair quickly by launching an amphibious assault against the island. But reducing the heavily fortified Nationalist positions would be quite costly, and the increased level of violence would only increase the political damage to Peking.

If Peking persevered in its interdiction, Quemoy would eventually fall. The consequences, however, would not necessarily be entirely favorable to Peking. The loss of so many Nationalist troops, many of them young conscripts from cities, villages, and farms in all parts of Taiwan, would

21. As a prelude to an assault on Taiwan, Peking might attack Quemoy and Matsu to eliminate the obstacle to the free use of the ports of Amoy and Foochow that the Nationalist garrisons on those islands pose.

22. In the 1958 crisis, when the mainland Chinese attempted a blockade of Quemoy, the U.S. Navy escorted supply ships to within three miles of Quemoy, an action that both sharply reduced the task of the Nationalist navy and constricted the operations of Communist naval and air units.

shatter morale. The Nationalist government would be blamed for the disaster, but rather than seek a negotiated settlement, as Peking might hope, Nationalist leaders (almost all from the mainland) might decide to share their power with the Taiwanese—and bring closer the day when Taiwan is governed by Taiwanese ready to declare their independence from the rest of China.

Whether or not the fall of Quemoy would push Taiwan toward independence, the symbolism of the capture of only a close-in offshore island would be all wrong for Peking's standing. The enormously greater difficulty of invading Taiwan would be underlined for the whole world to see. And the elimination of the only significant military front between Communist and Nationalist forces would signify an end to the civil war with the country still divided.

Blocking Supplies

A fourth military option open to Peking would be to cut off Taiwan's supply lines. Peking's navy and air force would not be able to establish an effective blockade, as that term is used in international law, but that would not be necessary. Peking could simply proclaim the closure of the ports and airfields of the province of Taiwan and, to obtain compliance, might even sink a ship or down a plane that approached Taiwan. High insurance rates and hazardous duty pay for voyages or flights to Taiwan would discourage further attempts.

The Nationalist navy and air force could not by itself counter interdiction. The navy does not have the antisubmarine capability to eliminate the threat to Taiwan's sea communications from Peking's submarines. And the air force could not establish the security north and south of Taiwan that would permit restoration of regular civil air service.

Loss of most air links with the outside world would be simply inconvenient and psychologically damaging. Loss of sea supply lines would be much more serious. The problem would not be the physical survival of the population (Taiwan grows a substantial part of its food, and essential imports, principally grain, could be brought in by naval convoy in ships of Taiwan registry); the problem would be massive unemployment and a precipitous fall in living standards.[23] Even more than Japan, Taiwan depends on imports, which it pays for by exporting industrial and agricul-

---

23. It is quite possible that, in deference to world opinion as well as for humanitarian reasons, Peking would not interfere with essential food imports.

tural products. In 1977, Taiwan's total imports were approximately 43 percent of its gross domestic product. Without imported fuel, raw ma-terials, and semifinished materials, much of Taiwan's industry would be unable to function and thousands of people would be out of work. Con-sumer goods would become increasingly hard to find for even those who still had cash incomes. Only the most severe government controls over dwindling fuel supplies could keep essential public services in operation.

How long Taiwan could endure these conditions before social and poli-tical disintegration began would depend on the quality of leadership and the resilience of the people. In the absence of outside intervention, how-ever, the island could probably be brought, in time, to a condition so disorganized as to make its seizure by forces from the mainland relatively easy.

The question is, of course, whether Peking would be allowed to apply its tactics without interference. Many nations whose trade, merchant ships, and civil aircraft would be affected could be expected to protest vigor-ously but to take no action, although direct action against the forces enforcing the closing order might be the only way to restore Taiwan's supply lines.

The United States would probably find such direct action necessary under the Mutual Defense Treaty with the Republic of China. Even in the absence of the treaty, the United States might decide to intervene in order to preserve the freedom of the seas and prevent forcible change in the status of Taiwan. If the United States did intervene, it would need suffi-cient antisubmarine capability to dispose of Peking's submarine fleet and sufficient air capability to enable the Nationalist air force to devote full attention to countering the air threat to civil aviation routes north and south of Taiwan.

Nuclear Proliferation

Three of the four nonnuclear-weapons states of Northeast Asia—Japan, the Republic of China, and the Republic of Korea—have the technical and economic means of acquiring nuclear weapons. (The capa-bilities of the fourth, North Korea, are more difficult to judge, but its policies are in any case less susceptible to influence by the United States.) Of the three, Japan could build nuclear weapons most quickly and, more-over, could develop both a large nuclear-armed force and more sophisti-cated delivery systems than the others.

Japan is at a severe strategic disadvantage regarding nuclear threats. The greater proportion of Japan's population and industry is concentrated in a narrow band on the Pacific coast of Honshu Island extending from Tokyo west to Osaka. A nuclear strike in this region would be devastating. Japan has no nuclear weapons of its own with which to threaten counter-strikes, no defense against ballistic missiles, and only an uncertain defense against nuclear-armed bombers. (This is not to say that a nuclear strike against Japan is probable. The Soviet Union's massive arsenal of nuclear delivery systems, while capable of striking Japan, is directed primarily at the United States and secondarily at China. And since China's embryonic nuclear capability is evolving in the context of Sino-Soviet hostilities, Japan is not a likely Chinese target.)

Nevertheless, Japan has eschewed the development of nuclear weapons. It relies instead on the deterrent power of the U.S. global nuclear retaliatory capability, tied to Japan's security by the U.S.-Japanese Mutual Security Treaty. During 1976, Japan reaffirmed in two ways its commitment to this policy. First, the Japan Defense Agency reiterated a reliance on the U.S. global nuclear deterrent and proclaimed Japan's continued adherence to three nonnuclear principles: "not to possess, not to manufacture, and not to allow the entry of nuclear weapons into this nation."[24] Second, in May 1976 the Japanese Diet ratified the Treaty on the Non-Proliferation of Nuclear Weapons, which includes among its provisions an agreement not to possess, manufacture, or acquire nuclear weapons.

Ratification of the nonproliferation treaty was not routine, however. It required six years from the time Japan signed the treaty in 1970 until it was ratified by the Japanese Diet. Although the delay was caused in large part by parliamentary maneuvering, the debate did reveal a sentiment among some factions for holding open the option of developing nuclear weapons.[25]

Those who opposed ratification of the pact did so for varying reasons. The Japanese Communist party represented the treaty as a vehicle by which the major powers could dominate nonnuclear nations. A minority faction of the ruling Liberal Democratic party opposed ratification on grounds more obviously related to Japan's defense: in an unpredictable world, Japan should not "abandon the freedom of option as to nuclear armament for a long time in the future."[26] A corollary concern, made ex-

---

24. Japan Defense Agency, *Defense of Japan 1976* (Tokyo: JDA, 1976), p. 32.
25. See John E. Endicott, "The 1975–76 Debate Over Ratification of the NPT in Japan," *Asian Survey,* vol. 17 (March 1977), pp. 275–92.
26. *Asahi Shimbun,* April 23, 1975.

plicit by some members of this faction, was that it was imprudent for Japan to rely in the long run entirely upon the United States for its security. One member of the upper house of the Diet even claimed, "if a nuclear bomb were to be dropped on Japan again I even think that it might be a U.S. nuclear bomb."[27] This opinion seems to be based on the belief that as competition between Japan and the United States over raw materials and export markets intensifies, there will be great potential for hostilities between the two—a view that is surely extreme even within the Liberal Democratic hawk faction. Notably, neither the Communists nor the Liberal Democratic minority advocated a nuclear weapons development program—which, if not necessarily a reflection of their preference, reflects a judgment that such a program would lack popular support.

Those voting for ratification did so for a variety of reasons:

1. *Public opinion.* A public opinion poll published in January 1976 revealed that 51 percent of those queried supported ratification of the nonproliferation treaty, while only 17 percent were opposed.[28]

2. *Economic considerations.* The United States and Canada, the two major suppliers of nuclear fuel to Japan, urged ratification. Concern over future nuclear fuel supplies from these nations made the case for ratification more compelling.

3. *Foreign policy considerations.* Hesitation over ratification was seen as damaging Japan's good relations with the United States and its image among other Asian nations as an unarmed superpower pursuing peaceful diplomacy.

4. *Strategic considerations.* Though not articulated, the strategic disadvantages to Japan's possession of nuclear weapons may have been recognized. A limited nuclear arsenal could become an incentive and a target for a preemptive nuclear strike during times of heightened tensions. Moreover, whatever the cost to its enemies, the cost to Japan of a nuclear exchange is likely to be far greater. Japan's concentrated population and industry would make a nuclear strike devastating. On the other hand, the populations and industries of Japan's conceivable adversaries, the Soviet Union and China, are dispersed.

In May 1976 these arguments carried the day. Dependence on the U.S. security guarantee was judged preferable even to keeping open the option to develop nuclear weapons. The issue will continue to deserve close attention from the United States, however. Japan's combination of modest

27. *Sankei Shimbun,* March 15, 1975.
28. Ibid., January 1, 1976.

military capability and great economic strength is the exception in the modern world and could prove vulnerable to external shocks. Japan has the economic capacity and technological expertise to build nuclear weapons. But the stakes are high. China and the smaller Asian nations would be alarmed by a nuclear-armed Japan, and pressure on the latter to acquire their own nuclear weapons would intensify.

There is much that the international community, the United States in particular, can do to make the nonnuclear option continue to be the more attractive. As long as the United States is viewed as a reliable and capable ally, Japan is not likely to feel the threat to its security that could be a prelude to a decision to develop nuclear weapons. In the absence of such a threat, the political, economic, and diplomatic incentives for maintaining the present posture should continue to be compelling.

Much the same conclusion is justified in the cases of South Korea and Nationalist China. Both rely on the U.S. nuclear umbrella, and both may need U.S. help in repelling conventional attacks. If either loses confidence in U.S. security commitments, a nuclear weapons capability may become an attractive, if somewhat desperate, option. Taking that option even while security treaties with the United States remain in full force might appear to some in Seoul and Taipei as a form of insurance. Thus far, however, other considerations have countervailed. First, both Seoul and Taipei have ratified the nonproliferation treaty. Second, both realize that violating or denouncing the treaty would be a sure way to weaken, if not destroy, the U.S. security commitment. And finally, the United States has many forms of leverage, including the interruption of nuclear fuel supplies, that could be used to make a decision to acquire nuclear weapons less attractive.

The question in the context of this study is whether specific U.S. force deployments influence the policies of Japan, South Korea, and Nationalist China toward nuclear weapons. In all probability, they do not, as long as these deployments deal with perceived threats and if changes in deployments are not handled in ways that imply a serious weakening of the U.S. security commitment.

CHAPTER FOUR

AN ALTERNATIVE FORCE STRUCTURE
FOR THE UNITED STATES

Not only are the U.S. military forces in Northeast Asia more than adequate to deal with the problems the United States faces in that part of the world, some appear to be in excess of clearly identifiable military requirements.

Ground forces of the U.S. allies are capable of coping with military contingencies, and U.S. ground units are required only for specialized intelligence, communications, and logistics in South Korea and for coping with such emergencies as the seizure of a U.S. ship. In terms of the primary naval threat—submarine interdiction of supply lines—a portion of the strength of the U.S. Navy in the Pacific is redundant. Some missions carried out by the carrier task force can be fulfilled by other units that are at present underutilized. The principal requirement for U.S. air power is compensation for the numerical advantage of the North Korean air force over the South Korean air force. Furthermore, U.S. air power is a component of the defense of Japan, and it might be required also in certain contingencies with respect to Taiwan. The U.S. air units now in the area plus one of the carrier task forces and one or two U.S. Marine Corps LHA assault ships armed with V/STOL aircraft deployed in the western Pacific appear sufficient to meet any likely requirements.

This chapter is therefore concerned with three questions. First, what might a U.S. force posture in Northeast Asia look like that was more closely adjusted to military requirements? Second, are there political obstacles or risks that might make moving to such a new force posture unwise? And, third, do strategic considerations beyond Northeast Asia argue for or against the alternative force posture?

An alternative force posture can be best set forth in three parts: naval forces, forces in Korea, and forces in Japan. (It is assumed that, consistent with the 1972 Shanghai Communiqué, no U.S. forces will be stationed in Taiwan.)[1] Having been spelled out, the alternative force posture can then be evaluated politically and strategically.

Naval Forces

Table 4-1 shows the 1978 U.S. naval forces in the western Pacific and an alternative for 1983 and 1988. Principal changes are the elimination of one carrier group (a carrier and escorts) and the introduction of the five new assault landing ships armed with V/STOL aircraft. (Eliminating one of the carrier groups in the western Pacific would release two of the four backup carrier groups in the eastern Pacific. It must be recognized, however, that the smaller backup force would have a greatly reduced surge capability and would also be less able to cope with unexpected contingencies, such as an accident.)

Table 4-1. U.S. Naval Forces in the Pacific, 1978, and Alternative Force, 1983 and 1988

Type of ship	1978	1983	1988
Aircraft carriers	6	3[a]	3[a]
Assault ships (LHA) with V/STOL aircraft	0	3[b]	5[b]
Surface combatants	87	75	75
Nuclear-powered attack submarines	26	31	36
Diesel-powered attack submarines	9	5	0
P-3C antisubmarine aircraft	36	36	36
Other amphibious ships[c]	27	25	24

Sources: 1978, Barry M. Blechman and Robert Berman, eds., *Guide to Far Eastern Navies* (Naval Institute Press, 1978), ch. 1, and unpublished data from the U.S. Department of the Navy, January 1977; 1983 and 1988, authors' recommendations.

a. Includes one at Yokosuka, Japan.

b. Includes at least one in Asian waters at all times.

c. Helicopter landing platforms, dock landing ships, tank landing ships.

One step the United States and Japan should take to minimize the impact of a Soviet interdiction of Japan's supply lines is timely mining or blockading of the exits from the Soviet bases in the Sea of Japan. The primary assistance the United States could render is supplemental air cover for Japan's convoys and U.S. antisubmarine forces to wage a war of attri-

1. The communiqué was issued at the conclusion of President Nixon's first visit to China and included the declaration that U.S. military forces on Taiwan would be progressively reduced as tension in the area eased and that the ultimate U.S. objective was to withdraw all U.S. forces from the island ("Text of Joint Communiqué Issued at Shanghai, February 27," *Department of State Bulletin,* vol. 66, p. 438).

tion against those Soviet submarines deployed at the time of the blockade. While carriers can contribute to these missions, alternative resources are available.

Air Cover

Japanese convoys approaching Japan from Indonesia would need cover while operating within range of Soviet aircraft, roughly to the Philippine Sea. U.S. air force units operating from the Philippines, Japan, and possibly from Korea, could supplement Japanese air self-defense units. Reduced carrier protection, however, might jeopardize access to some of those fields.[2]

Antisubmarine Warfare

The resources most useful in tracking down and destroying Soviet submarines are the U.S. Navy's nuclear-powered attack submarines (SSNs), P-3C antisubmarine warfare (ASW) aircraft, and surface escorts with active sonar and the increasingly effective passive towed-array systems. Assignment of a submarine to operate with each Japanese convoy (four convoys are probably sufficient) would enhance the defense but would not impose a serious drain on the force of twenty-six SSNs assigned to the U.S. Pacific Fleet. In addition, the four squadrons of nine P-3C ASW aircraft in the western Pacific could be reinforced by the eight squadrons on the West Coast and in Hawaii. Several P-C3s could operate with the convoys to extend the antisubmarine screen about the convoy. Moreover, Japan's Maritime Self Defense Force (MSDF) is acquiring forty-five P-3C aircraft.[3] Surface units with active sonar remain essential to any convoy escort task.[4]

2. The Soviet Tu-26 bomber (Backfire) could be countered by the U.S. air superiority fighter, the F-15 Eagle.

3. Barry Wheeler, "World's Air Forces 1978," *Flight International,* vol. 114 (July 8, 1978), p. 128.

4. Both SSNs and P-3s search with passive sensors, which work only when an enemy submarine makes noise. Without active sonars, enemy submarines could lie still in the path of the convoy and be undetectable. U.S. surface ships would be required to operate with U.S. P-3 and SSN units for command and control reasons. Under the stress of tactical situations, P-3 and SSN commanders may not operate comfortably within weapon range of friendly foreign surface units because of differences in language and procedures. The presence of U.S. surface units would alleviate such confusion.

Landing Forces

To supplement the carrier presence, one of the two marine battalion landing teams now maintained afloat in the western Pacific could operate on an LHA carrying Harrier V/STOL (vertical or short takeoff and landing) aircraft. A typical loading could include eighteen Harriers and about sixteen medium-lift and heavy-lift helicopters to support assault operations.[5]

Three LHAs would need to be assigned to the Pacific to keep one deployed forward continuously. With five, a second LHA could be deployed forward periodically. Each LHA deployed forward requires an escort of at least two surface combatants, probably a destroyer and a frigate. This requirement could easily be met by the forces projected for the Pacific in the 1980s.

The launch of the third LHA (*Belleau Wood*) is scheduled for January 1979; and estimating a year beyond launch date for full operational capability, it will be 1980 before a rotation of three LHAs, with one continuously forward, could be established. In the meantime, the LHA-1 *Tarawa* and the LHA-2 *Saipan* could deploy forward occasionally in lieu of an aircraft carrier. Three of the Pacific carriers could begin their transfer to the Atlantic by 1980 and complete it by 1983. The gradual phasing into the Pacific of the LHA configured as a V/STOL carrier would permit reassessment of the policy over about a five-year period.

Since its air defenses are less sophisticated than those of an aircraft carrier, the LHA is best used far from Soviet air bases (the waters south of Japan, the waters around Southeast Asia, and the Indian Ocean).[6] The

5. The Marine Corps helicopter landing ships support a battalion landing team with twenty-six CH-46 Sea Knight medium-lift helicopters on board: the LHA has room for thirty-two CH-46s. Alternatively, an LHA could carry eighteen Harriers (which require only slightly more space than a CH-46), plus eight CH-53 Sea Stallion heavy-lift helicopters and eight CH-46s. While the CH-53 requires about 50 percent more space than a CH-46, it has three times the lift capacity, and this arrangement would result in only a minimal reduction in assault capability.

6. The AV-8B advanced Harrier, requested by the U.S. Marine Corps, will have provision for four air-to-air or air-to-ground missiles (the AV-8A can carry two) and it will have improved speed and maneuverability. It will not have an intercept capability comparable to the F-14 and F-4 aircraft operated from aircraft carriers. The Marine Corps' plan is to replace its current light attack force with eight squadrons of AV-8Bs. The Department of Defense, however, has recommended reduced funding of the program, which could delay production and lead to cancellation. As of mid-1978 it appears likely that Congress will restore funds to ensure continuation of the program (*Department of Defense Appropriation Bill, 1979*, H. Rept. 95-1398, 95 Cong. 2 sess. [GPO, 1978], pp. 338–40).

reduced capability of its aircraft component relative to a conventional aircraft carrier is in part offset by the capability of the marine combat troops on board. Troops that can go ashore can respond better than air and seapower to some crises (for example, evacuating U.S. citizens threatened by civil disorder or dealing with an incident such as the seizure of the *Mayaguez*). The marines aboard the LHA could come from units located in Hawaii or the West Coast, if those now on Okinawa are withdrawn.

As the LHAs come into service, parallel developments in V/STOL technology will enhance their flexibility. The AV-8B advanced Harrier, scheduled for full production in 1983 and initial operational capability in 1984, will be able to carry an ordnance load greater than the conventional A-4, now in service. In addition, the Navy plans to develop V/STOL antisubmarine and airborne early warning (AEW) aircraft, and these too could operate from an LHA, extending its range of ASW surveillance and enhancing its air defenses.

Forces in Korea

Table 4-2 summarizes an alternative U.S. military deployment in Korea. It is similar in many respects to the program announced by the Carter

Table 4-2. U.S. Military Personnel in Korea, 1978, and Alternative Force, 1983 and 1988

Type of force	1978	1983	1988
Army	**32,600**	**7,000**	**1,000**
Combat	15,000[a]	0	0
Logistics	4,800[b]	3,000[c]	0
Communications, surveillance, and intelligence	3,500[d]	3,500	500[e]
Other	9,300	500[f]	500[f]
Air	**7,600**	**7,600**	**7,600**
Navy and Marine	**600**[f]	**600**[f]	**600**[f]
Total	**40,800**	**14,800**	**8,800**

Sources: 1978, Hubert H. Humphrey and John Glenn, *U.S. Troop Withdrawal from the Republic of Korea*, a report to the Senate Committee on Foreign Relations, 95 Cong. 2 sess. (Government Printing Office, 1978); and U.S. Department of Defense, Office of the Secretary of Defense, "DOD Military Personnel Strength by Regional Area and Country" (March 28, 1978); 1983 and 1988, authors' recommendations.
a. U.S. Army Second Division.
b. Includes Nineteenth Support Brigade, Second Transportation Company, and Second Engineering Group.
c. Primarily equipment maintenance and overhaul personnel.
d. Includes First Signal Brigade and intelligence personnel.
e. Includes only intelligence personnel and a skeleton crew of advisors.
f. Joint U.S.-Korea military advisory group and liaison personnel.

administration in the summer of 1977: the withdrawal of the U.S. Army Second Division between 1978 and 1982 and gradual reductions in U.S. logistic, communications, surveillance, and intelligence personnel. In addition, most but not all of the tactical nuclear weapons would be withdrawn. No change is proposed in U.S. Air Force strength. The alternative would maintain a stable balance of power on the Korean peninsula.

Ground Forces

The removal of the Second Division will not affect greatly the balance of ground forces. South Korea's total armed forces outnumber those of the North. With some enhancement of the South's firepower (see below), neither army would have a clear edge over the other. On the other hand, removal of U.S. combat troops from their position astride the invasion corridor will reduce the risk to North Korea of immediate and automatic involvement of U.S. ground forces in any Korean conflict. This specter enhances the deterrent value of the Second Division beyond that derived from its intrinsic military capabilities, and its removal will lessen the overall deterrent to attack by the North—and argues for a cautious withdrawal.

Air Forces

Upon completion of the force improvement plan (originally scheduled for 1980 but currently running two years behind), the South Korean Air Force should be a formidable opponent for the North—unless the Soviet Union provides the North with its newest generation of fighter and attack aircraft or unless the North launches massive surprise attacks at the outset of a conflict, making its quantitative edge too telling an advantage to be neutralized by South Korea's air force and missile air defenses.

Given these possibilities, there are two choices open to the United States: cooperate with South Korea in building its air force further than now planned or keep the sixty U.S. tactical fighters (F-4D/Es) in the South. There are two reasons the second option is the more desirable. (1) The air wing is a major U.S. military unit, and its presence in Korea serves as a continued reassurance to the South and a warning to the North of the U.S. commitment to the defense of South Korea. (2) With U.S. tactical air support, South Korea can apply its resources to upgrading defenses against ground attack (for example, antiarmor and artillery firepower).

Thus the South would be restrained from building an air force so strong that it would be tempted to take offensive action against the North. Moreover, the United States can eventually replace the F-4 with the more capable F-16.

Support Forces, Antisubmarine Forces, and Munitions

When South Korea rebuilt its armed forces following the Korean War, it emphasized combat units and neglected support units. While this would have little effect during the opening days of war, it would affect the tide of battle as the staying power of South Korean forces was weakened by thin logistic support. However, the U.S. Army Nineteenth Support Brigade and Second Transportation Company, which now provide logistic support to the U.S. Eighth Army and the Second Division, could remain in South Korea while the division is leaving, to train South Koreans to operate a logistics network capable of supporting combat elements.

South Korea does have the assets to haul most combat materiel to the front—in wartime, civilian trucks would also be mobilized—and the Second Transportation Company could help it to organize a transportation network and to take over U.S. army operations at the port of Pusan. These tasks should be completed by 1982, when the last U.S. ground combat forces are expected to depart.

The Nineteenth Support Brigade, which maintains and overhauls military equipment, could train South Koreans to perform these functions. The task would be complex and progress could be expected to be gradual, so U.S. personnel might be needed for three years after the withdrawal of the division. Maintenance of some support personnel in Korea is part of the administration's plan.

The U.S. Army operates very sophisticated electronic equipment to gather intelligence, maintain surveillance of North Korean activities, provide early warning of air attack, and provide theater-wide communications. At present, the pool of ROK personnel with the requisite technical skills from which to draw trainees for these functions is limited. As South Korea's economy develops and its technological base expands, more South Koreans will develop the technical expertise needed to replace U.S. personnel. Until that time—perhaps ten years from now—these functions must be performed by the First Signal Brigade and by intelligence specialists. (This option is favored by the Carter administration.)

The ROK navy and rear-area security forces have the resources to prevent large-scale North Korean amphibious attacks and infiltration. The South's antisubmarine capabilities are limited, however, and the North's eight submarines could affect efforts to resupply the South with war materiel. U.S. navy antisubmarine assets, particularly the squadrons of P-3C aircraft in the western Pacific, would be necessary (and sufficient) to prevent a blockade of Pusan. In addition, the U.S. Seventh Fleet's combat and antisubmarine aircraft could be brought to the conflict.

A forward defense against an intense North Korean assault aimed at Seoul would require a rapid expenditure of munitions, and the stocks now in place may not be adequate. To increase these stocks, the United States could assist the South in establishing its own munitions industry. The requisite technical expertise is well within the capabilities of South Korean industry. Although artillery pieces are more difficult to manufacture— and cannot be manufactured in the near future—the South's deficiency could be alleviated if the Second Division's approximately eighty artillery pieces were left in Korea.[7]

Nuclear Deterrence

The United States should eventually remove the land-based and air-delivered tactical nuclear weapons positioned in South Korea. (A stable balance of conventional military forces can be maintained on the peninsula if, as discussed above, the United States supports ROK forces in areas where they are deficient.) If the strong deterrent signal of nuclear weapons were deemed advisable during times of heightening tension, a carrier with nuclear-armed aircraft could be brought into Korean waters. The tactical nuclear weapons in the hands of U.S. army units should be removed during the period in which the Second Division is being withdrawn. The removal of nuclear weapons that are now in the hands of air force units should be deferred until the full effects of the withdrawal of the Second Division is assessed.

Of major concern is that removing U.S. nuclear weapons might spur South Korea to develop its own—with the destabilizing consequence of inducing North Korea and possibly Japan to develop their own. To avoid this situation, the United States should use its considerable leverage to discourage any steps by the South that could lead to a nuclear capability: the United States is South Korea's primary supplier of advanced military

7. U.S. Department of the Army, *Armor Reference Data, FY 1976,* vol. 1 (Fort Knox, Kentucky: DOA, 1976), ST 17-1-1.

equipment and spare parts; it provides South Korea with air and naval support; and only the United States can offset the political support North Korea receives from China and the Soviet Union. U.S. influence has already been evident in South Korea's decisions to ratify the nuclear nonproliferation treaty and to scrap plans to acquire a nuclear reprocessing facility, which would have yielded plutonium usable in nuclear weapons.

Command Arrangement

Withdrawal of U.S. ground troops will almost certainly lead to changes in command arrangements. South Korea cannot be expected to keep its forces under a UN command headed by a U.S. general, when the command will no longer include any U.S. or other foreign ground forces. Dissolution of the UN command would raise the question of who should represent the non-Communist side in carrying out the armistice agreement and would eliminate the formal authority of the United States over South Korea forces in crises with the North. But as long as both sides want the armistice to continue, the procedural requirements can certainly be met. And U.S. influence in South Korea is based more on ROK dependence on U.S. air, naval, and logistic support than on the theoretical authority of the UN commander over ROK forces.

Forces in Japan

Table 4-3 sets forth the alternative force posture in Japan. The principal changes are withdrawal of the third Marine Division, which (minus

Table 4-3. U.S. Military Personnel in Japan, 1978, and Alternative Force, 1983 and 1988

Type of force	1978	1983	1988
Marine	21,000[a]	21,000[a]	0[b]
Air	14,000	14,000	14,000
Navy	8,000	8,000	8,000
Army	4,000	4,000	4,000
Total	47,000	47,000	26,000

Sources: 1978 estimates based on Japan Defense Agency, *Defense of Japan 1977*, p. 26; 1983 and 1988, authors' recommendations.

a. Includes 13,000 in Third Division and 8,000 in First Air Wing.

b. About 3,000 Marines would be maintained afloat in the western Pacific along with elements of the First Air Wing operating Harrier aircraft from the LHA and LPH ships in the region.

one regimental landing team) is stationed in Okinawa, and the First Marine Air Wing, now based at Iwakuni in western Honshu.

The withdrawal of the Third Division is justified by the lack of any clear mission other than responding to small emergencies, which could be performed by two battalion-sized landing teams deployed afloat in the western Pacific. In the event that U.S. ground forces were needed to help repel a North Korean attack on South Korea, army or marine units from Hawaii or the continental United States could be moved quickly by air. Withdrawal of the marine aircraft is proposed on the ground that they should be based near the two marine divisions they support, neither of which would be in the western Pacific under the alternative force posture.

These ground and air forces should be withdrawn over a period of several years, the exact time depending on reactions to other aspects of the new force posture, particularly reactions to the withdrawal of ground combat forces from Korea.

No changes are proposed in air force units or in land-based naval forces; they are needed to aid Japan's air defense, to reinforce the U.S. Air Force in Korea, and to facilitate operations of the Seventh Fleet in Northeast Asia. The small number of army personnel engaged in logistic, liaison, and base maintenance would also remain.

Political Considerations

The political consequences of shifting to the alternative force depends principally on how the change is perceived by the nations of Northeast Asia. In the worst case, these nations would see the withdrawal of U.S. ground combat forces and the reduction in U.S. naval strength as evidence of declining U.S. interest in the area and would question the will and ability of the United States to honor its security commitments and to prevent an expansion of Soviet influence.

This worst-case perception would affect the countries of Northeast Asia in various ways, all of them contrary to U.S. interests.

North Korea would see less risk in attacking South Korea, and South Korea would have less confidence in its ability to repel an attack. Even if war did not break out, tension between North Korea and South Korea would mount, chances for accommodation between them would diminish, and political strains within South Korea would probably increase.

Japan would be concerned over developments in Korea and, more important, would feel isolated and helpless in the face of Soviet power, leading it to reexamine both its ties with the United States and its own security policies. The most likely alternative to present policies would be a heavily armed neutrality, possibly including a nuclear-weapons capability. Even in the event Japan shrunk from so drastic a change, the debate over how it could survive in an increasingly threatening environment could bring to power political elements with little interest in continuing Japan's cooperative relation with the United States.

The reactions of Peking and Taipei would to some extent parallel those of Pyongyang and Seoul. Military action by mainland forces against Taiwan would become more likely, but the most important consequence could be in the triangular relation among China, the Soviet Union, and the United States. Diminution of U.S. interest and power in the area might encourage the Soviet Union to apply pressure on China and might make China feel more exposed and vulnerable. This situation could only worsen Sino-Soviet relations and either increase the risk of war between them or force a partial accommodation between them, with China making most of the concessions. If one of those concessions were Soviet use of Chinese ports for its submarine fleet, the United States and Japan, in some future crisis, could not as readily bottle up a substantial part of that fleet in the Sea of Japan.

These worst-case consequences need not happen. If the United States bolstered South Korean defense capabilities, as described above, it would at the same time reinforce the deterrent to North Korean attack and increase South Korean self-confidence. Also, the United States would still have the wherewithal to show impressive strength. For example, following the axe murder of U.S. soldiers at Panmunjon in August 1976, the United States brought to Korea a squadron of F-4s from Okinawa, a squadron of F-111s from Idaho, three B-52s from Guam, and the carrier *Midway* from Japan. These and others, particularly air force units, will still be available after the Second Division is withdrawn and could respond rapidly in the event of heightened tensions on the peninsula.

These capabilities should also be demonstrated during less tense times; U.S. forces should be highly visible in the region after the ground combat troops are withdrawn. A U.S. carrier task force could frequent Korean waters; and joint U.S.-ROK military exercises should expand. The U.S. air force units in Korea now train regularly with the ROK air force; these exercises could also include aircraft from U.S. squadrons outside Korea and even aircraft from the United States. (A precedent for the latter were the joint exercises in May 1976, which included a squadron of F-111 aircraft deployed from Mountain Home Air Force Base, Idaho.) A battalion or brigade-sized detachment of U.S. marines could move from the West Coast to Korea and would be a highly visible replacement for the Second Division as the U.S. component of Focus Lens, the annual joint U.S.-ROK training maneuvers. In addition, the carrier *Midway* should remain based at Yokosuka, Japan, and its operations should be concentrated in Northeast Asian waters; one or two marine battalion landing teams should be deployed on assault landing ships (LHA) with a complement of V/STOL fighter aircraft and maintained afloat in the western Pacific region; and any training exercise involving the U.S. Navy and Japan's Maritime Self Defense Force should also include U.S. and Japanese air force units.

Because it is impossible to know whether measures such as these will reduce political damage to an acceptable level, it is prudent to move to the new force posture in stages (like the gradual withdrawal of ground forces from Korea), testing reactions at each stage. But even gradualism in execution might not be enough to reduce the inherent risks to acceptable levels. The stakes are high: maintenance of peace and the future of U.S. relations with two of the most important countries in the world, Japan and China.

Strategic Considerations

From a narrowly regional point of view, the military arguments for moving to the alternative force structure may be canceled by the political risks, and objective observers may differ over the balance of advantages and disadvantages. In the broad strategic context, however, the wisdom of adopting the alternative force structure is made plain. The proposed withdrawal of ground forces and the reduction in naval strength would not represent a diminution of U.S. military capabilities globally. On the contrary, the units would presumably be kept in being and made available to support U.S. policy in Europe and the Mediterranean, to shore up defenses against Soviet armed forces.

A shift in U.S. naval deployments from the Pacific to the Atlantic is especially important. There is no pressing strategic reason to maintain approximately half the U.S. Navy, including six of the twelve carrier groups, in the Pacific. The U.S. Navy appears to be harder pressed by the

Soviet navy in the Mediterranean and Atlantic regions than in the Pacific.[8] Moreover, the number of ships in the U.S. Navy continues to decline.

About 70 percent of the Soviet Union's naval forces are assigned to its three western fleets, which are equipped with more modern ships and aircraft than its Far East Fleet. Moreover, the Soviet navy is much more active in the Atlantic Ocean and Mediterranean Sea than in the Pacific and Indian Oceans. Its average daily combined deployments (1976) of aircraft carriers, attack submarines, surface combat ships, amphibious ships, and mine warfare ships, compared below with U.S. deployments are:[9]

Ocean	U.S. ships	Soviet ships
Mediterranean	33	25
Atlantic	22	12
Indian	4	8
Pacific	40	2

During a crisis in the Middle East or Europe, the power of the U.S. Navy to influence events in the eastern Mediterranean would be challenged by the concentration of Soviet naval power. If the United States and the Soviet Union agree to limit naval deployments in the Indian Ocean, requirements now met by the U.S. Seventh Fleet would be reduced. Given the asymmetry between Soviet and U.S. naval forces in the Pacific (and the lack of serious naval threat from any other nation), three U.S. carriers and about twelve escorts might be reassigned to the Atlantic—enhancing the navy's strength in the Mediterranean and North Atlantic. One of the three carrier groups could be deployed permanently forward or could be used to improve the surge capability of the U.S. Atlantic Fleet in the event of an Arab-Israeli crisis or heightened tension between the NATO and Warsaw Pact nations.

The reassignment would reduce from two to one the number of carrier groups the U.S. Pacific Fleet can deploy forward continuously. It would not, however, affect the resources available to the U.S. Pacific Fleet in a war with the Soviet Union: three of the six carrier groups would in any case be stripped from the Pacific force and redeployed to the Atlantic.

The army division withdrawn from Korea could be stationed in the

8. See Barry M. Blechman et al., "Toward a New Consensus in U.S. Defense Policy," in Henry Owen and Charles L. Schultze, eds., *Setting National Priorities: The Next Ten Years* (Brookings Institution, 1976).

9. U.S. Department of Defense, Office of the Secretary of Defense, "U.S. Defense Perspectives, Fiscal Year 1978" (DOD, 1977).

continental United States, where it would be readily available for deployment to Europe. The Third Marine Division might well be consolidated on Hawaii, where one of its three regiments is already located. The army division now on Hawaii could then be moved to the continental United States, adding its strength to the units positioned for possible deployment to Europe.

The Third Marine Division in Hawaii and the First Marine Division in California could assume responsibility for any contingencies short of large-scale war requiring the use of U.S. ground forces in Northeast Asia and the Pacific. These divisions could supply the two landing teams afloat in the western Pacific, one, and occasionally both, on an LHA configured as a V/STOL carrier.

The strong strategic justifications for moving military strength, especially naval, from the Pacific to the Atlantic might moderate adverse political reactions to the move in Northeast Asia. Peking in particular has shown concern for the strength of NATO and would probably see merit in an action that would strengthen defenses against the Soviet Union in Europe.

Conclusion

The U.S. military force posture in Northeast Asia is wasteful, employing units not needed to meet the military requirements of the region. A posture matching forces and requirements calls for no ground combat forces permanently stationed in Asia, the forward deployment of only one carrier group, and one and occasionally two LHA V/STOL carriers replacing the second carrier group.

Moving to a rationalized force posture involves large political risks. These risks might be reduced by actions that countered the perception that the United States intended to withdraw from Northeast Asia and the western Pacific. Moving to the new force posture by gradual stages might also soften the adverse political effects.

From a narrow regional point of view, the political risks may outweigh the military gains. But from a broad strategic point of view, the case for rationalizing the U.S. military force structure in Northeast Asia is strong.

DATE DUE

GAYLORD			PRINTED IN U.S.A.